THE COMPLETE BOOK OF
PAINT
TECHNIQUES

THE COMPLETE BOOK OF
PAINT
TECHNIQUES

Penny Swift · Janek Szymanowski

In collaboration with Martine Criticos and Keryn Paull

NH

NEW
HOLLAND

First published in 1994 by
New Holland (Publishers) Ltd
London • Cape Town • Sydney • Singapore

Reprinted 1995, 1996

24 Nutford Place
London W1H 6DQ
UK

P.O. Box 1144
Cape Town 8000
South Africa

3/2 Aquatic Drive
Frenchs Forest, NSW 2086
Australia

ISBN 1 85368 294 2 (hbk)
ISBN 1 85368 306 X (pbk)

Editor: Coral Walker
Designer: Janice Evans

Typeset by Ace Filmsetting Ltd, Frome, Somerset
Reproduction by Hirt & Carter (Pty) Ltd
Printed and bound in Singapore by Kyodo Printing Co (Pte) Ltd

*A gentle combination of dusky pink vinyl matt emulsion
on the walls and pale leaf green eggshell on the door frame
and floorboards makes for a tranquil bedroom.*

CONTENTS

INTRODUCTION

Paint is a magical decorating tool. Relatively cheap, universally accessible, and extraordinarily versatile, it places a whole new world within easy reach. Today an enormous range of paint is available for domestic use, offering a sometimes overwhelming choice.

Developed with the two distinct functions of protection and decoration in mind, paint enables us to protect the surfaces inside and outside our homes and at the same time embellish our environment. A wonderful source of colour, paint offers endless possibilities for the unskilled home decorator and professional interior designer alike. For many people, this is where it ends. But the discovery of broken colour and decorative paint finishes reveals that this is just the beginning.

Following a huge international revival, a rapidly increasing number of people are using numerous decorative paint techniques in shops, offices, restaurants and homes. These range from simple sponging and colourwashing to intricate stencilling and bravura marbling.

The more outrageously imaginative approaches are understandably usually limited to commercial situations, all of which benefit from the public enthusiasm adventurous paint finishes generate. Star-studded ceilings, marbled or granite-spattered floors, trompe l'oeil Persian wall hangings, ambitious murals and decadent distressing never fail to illicit comment from customers and clients.

At the same time, some of the most exclusive homes have a touch of technique on walls, floors, ceilings and furniture alike. Mostly these are professionally painted interiors, transformed by an exclusive body of artists and craftsmen operating under the skilful guidance of qualified interior designers. Given entrée to these houses, one sees a refreshing range of décor, with exquisite paint finishes adding to patterns and texture as well as to colour.

In an age of fast technology and massive consumerism, there is a nostalgic yearning for times past when the pace of life was slower and more peaceable. As with every generation, we know that many things viewed retrospectively take on a rosy tinge and the notion that life was somehow of a better quality. Witness the Victorians' love of the medieval and their romanticizing of Arthurian legend. Yet, in truth this image is wildly inaccurate as the Middle Ages were largely an extremely brutal time.

However, this said, there is much to be learned from the times when craftsmanship was paramount and great individual care and skill was used in interior decoration.

Interestingly, the rapidly increasing popularity of paint techniques coincides with a huge restoration movement; and so one is seeing a new lease of life given to traditional techniques in museums and historic buildings too.

Although I knew about historic friezes and wall paintings, my own introduction to modern decorative paint finishes was a visit to a fabulous commercial building in 1985. But the relevance of these astonishing effects to domestic décor only dawned on me later when I saw four naïvely ragged wooden chairs in the home of a writer friend. Then I began to notice paint effects wherever I went. I found myself touching surfaces and exploring textures; absorbing and appreciating paint effects and fantasy finishes in every walk of life.

This book shares my discoveries and my own delight in finding that many decorative paint finishes can be successfully handled by amateur decorators. It also provides a brief background to interior decoration and decorative paint techniques over the years.

The wonderful collection of photographs, most taken especially for this book, provide visual inspiration for a multitude of applications. The selection of step-by-step photographs, together with detailed instructions, is aimed to guide you through the more popular techniques. In addition, I have included guidelines to readily available materials and equipment, offering tested substitutes for those which are costly or unnecessary. A selected list of suppliers and decorators is provided, along with a comprehensive reading list for those hungry for more.

Penny Swift

Fake marble pillars and a marbled floor are features of a glamorous women's boutique. Unusual décor with lavish drapes as well as a star-studded ceiling give it an air of opulence.

Part One
HISTORICAL PERSPECTIVES

The history of decorative painting provides one of the most fascinating studies in the field of interior design. Man's preoccupation with embellishing his environment goes beyond geographic and cultural boundaries and has influenced every era we can identify.

While it is sometimes difficult to trace accurately the origins or early development of specialist techniques, it does seem that many of the world's civilisations have practised forms of decorative painting for thousands of centuries.

In fact it seems that nothing much is new and that just about every definable technique has been tried before, although inevitably with different materials, tools and styles of application. At the same time, just like everything else, paint techniques are, and always have been, affected by fashion. So we discover eras during which the popularity of various finishes is obvious and then periods during which there is no evidence of their use at all. Perhaps the current revival will encourage us to learn more about the past.

The corner of this stately living room was originally painted in the eighteenth century. It shows trompe l'oeil pillars, faux panels and charming medallions.

ANTIQUITY

All things considered, much of what we do today stems from ancient arts and crafts. Wall paintings of various kinds have been found in many parts of the world: the oldest probably predating the birth of Christ by some 20,000 years.

Comparatively sophisticated animal wall paintings were done during the ice age, long, long ago. Incredibly, pigments like yellow ochre, black oxide of manganese, red iron oxide and white chalk were used together with animal fat and discovered thousands of years later, in vessels and on the walls of now famous caves like Altamira in Spain.

A look at prehistoric art shows that techniques, including stylised marbling and woodgraining, were found on ancient Greek (Mycenaean) pottery dating from 2200 BC. Decorative wall paintings were found in the tombs of ancient Egypt and fake graining was discovered to have been an accomplished craft as early as the third and fourth dynasties. Even stencilled silks dating from 1000 BC have been discovered in China, where this technique is believed to have originated before 300 BC.

WORLD HISTORY

As time goes on, we see a smattering of masterful techniques emerging the world over. How much still lies hidden, never to be revealed, we will never know. But it is fascinating to piece the bits together. For instance, a tragedy like the volcanic eruption of Mount Vesuvius in the year AD 79 provides us with some insight into the magnificent wall paintings of classical Rome. If prosperous Pompeii had not been buried in lava, we may never have discovered the incredible artistic fashions of that era. Excavations done over the centuries have uncovered friezes; trompe l'oeil panels, painted architraves and other illusionary architectural features; magnificent frescoes and painted marble in a series of baffling styles probably accomplished over some 150 years.

The Roman catacombs too, reveal wall paintings from the first few centuries after the birth of Christ. There is some written evidence of murals in Italy during the period AD 700–900, but most have vanished. However the country is rich with paintings done in later years: especially during the Renaissance (fourteenth to sixteenth centuries). This period produced some amazing works, the best known by Michelangelo and Leonardo da Vinci.

Travelling on through history, we find a re-emergence of the art of illusion in the age of Baroque: with trompe l'oeil features reminiscent of the Middle Ages – many of the painters covering huge ceiling areas in palaces and churches, impressively drawing on the traditional techniques of the past.

18th and 19th centuries

The 18th and 19th centuries really took interior decoration to new levels. Names which are still much referred to today, such as Robert Adam, Sir John Soane and William Morris, made great impact on design during this time, not only in England, but also across Europe and the colonies.

With the ending of the Baroque in the early 1700s came the Rococo age. Originating in France, this style made use of the rocaille motif which took the form of rocks and shells. The style was highly decorative with sensuous curves and swirling Arabesque frescoes and architecture.

The late 1700s are often thought of as eclectic to the point of messy, borrowing as they did from a wide variety of styles brought together from an even wider variety of sources. This eclecticism was made possible by the development of the railways and steam navigation. With more and better opportunities to travel, a number of exotic influences became accessible to a much wider public. There was heavy influence from Greece, Spain, India and North Africa as Arabian carpets and Eastern fabrics became immensely popular among the wealthy.

In fact, it was really only the wealthy that could afford many of the new decorating innovations and techniques of the day.

A pretty eighteenth century freize of roses adorns a panelled door.

William Morris (1834–1896)

At the middle of the 19th century, stands possibly one of the most influential interior designers, not just in Britain, but across the world: William Morris.

A committed socialist and poet, Morris's love of the medieval led him, when an undergraduate at Oxford University, to meet the charismatic Dante Gabriel Rossetti, a founder of the pre-Raphaelite movement in the mid-1800s.

Inspired by Rossetti, Morris eschewed a career in the Church, and went instead the way of the decorative arts. Just five years later in 1861 he founded Morris & Co to make decorations and furnishings of aesthetic appeal available to the public. The company existed, under various titles, for 80 years and many of his wallpaper and fabric designs are still available today.

Although, principally known for his textiles, wallpapers and stained glass, Morris's attitude to design is inspirational: 'However original a man may be, he cannot afford to disregard the works of art that have been produced in times past when design was flourishing . . . he is also bound to supplement that by a careful study of nature . . .

The success of William Morris led to a vast number of imitations, not just in Britain, but on the Continent and later in America where his designs were fervently greeted.

Morris was not alone in his love of the medieval, thus, it was common for the Victorians to romanticize anything from the Middle Ages and many Gothic styles and fantasies exist from this time.

DEVELOPMENT OF COLOUR

Before the mid-1700s, the most available pigments for decorating were generally of earthy hues. Hence, decoration until this time was largely in these 'natural' earth tones, with walls in 'stone' colours and woodwork in 'wood' colours. 'Wainscot' actually referred to a type of brown colour.

It wasn't until the close of the 18th century that stronger colours grew more in evidence as the development and manufacture of chemical colours took a dramatic leap forward. Events such as the discovery of Pompeiian and Etruscan antiquities coincidently brought about a surge of interest in bright vivid colours. And it is around this time that bright yellows, pea greens and red (known as Pompeiian red) were produced. In fact, these Pompeiian colour schemes continued well into the third quarter of the 19th century and are once again popular today.

Above: Early nineteenth century wall paintings designed to resemble wallpaper. Below: Stencilling from the period.

Colour manufacture continued at an ever growing pace throughout the 19th century which, together with widening distribution and expanded production, brought new exciting colours and shades into the hands of the fast growing middle classes.

By the close of the Victorian era, dark, heavy colours began to rapidly diminish in popularity. With the emergence of the Modern Movement in design and architecture, white and space came into their own. Many subtle shades of white were created using clever mixes of paints and glazes to give a merest hint of pink, ivory or cream. This was usually achieved by painting a coloured basecoat, and applying several coats of white glaze.

DEVELOPMENT OF PAINT TECHNIQUES

It is difficult to precisely track down when exactly certain techniques came into being. However, we owe much to the ancient Egyptians whose methods and materials came to Europe via the Greeks.

The Egyptians learned how to bind colour to wood, mortar and stone. Their colours were mixed with honey, gum, size, milk, wax and egg. For their walls, they simply mixed raw pigments with water and applied them directly on to the wet lime surface. This technique was later called 'fresco' by the Italians and has been in use ever since.

It is evident that the Egyptians discovered ways of 'faking' many decorative features which may have been expensive or difficult to obtain.

There is less known about the ancient Greeks, although they too worked in distemper and fresco. They made black by burning ivory, giving us the term ivory black.

The Romans copied the Greeks, but had added purple to the otherwise earth pigments of their palette. By the Middle Ages, ultramarine was in evidence, made from lapis lazuli.

Undoubtedly, the colours influenced the decor of the day; and as we have already seen, with the widening of the palette and the production of chemical colour, came an explosion in interior design for an ever-growing number of people.

Murals

Pictures as decorations – whether directly on to a wall or a piece of furniture – has always been an interior favourite. Early panelling was frequently decorated with pictures, even though it was good hardwood.

William Morris's hall cupboard at his Red House in Kent was decorated with scenes from Arthurian romance painted by his friend, the famous artist, Edward Burne-Jones. In fact, up until extremely recently, most murals were undertaken by artists or specialists.

Trompe l'oeil

Like murals, trompe l'oeil was often the only decorative feature of an otherwise plain wall or door. Panelling of the 16th century was frequently decorated in trompe l'oeil to imitate carvings. This type of trompe l'oeil was often used over the years and by the middle of the 19th century, realistic panelled effects were created by artists of some skill.

Trompe l'oeil friezes were often in the forms of drapes or fabric 'pelmets' and they were common in the 19th century along with fashionable wallpapers.

The secret of trompe l'oeil was to ensure all subjects were life size and complete. Thus, full-size French windows painted to

Above: More modern murals, commissioned around 50 years ago.
Below: Classically-inspired murals painted in the late eighteenth century. The medallion (left) contains a self-portrait of the artist, Jan Adam Hartman.

reveal a garden vista beyond worked well. Other successful trompe l'oeil subjects included small shelves cluttered with books and paintings of paintings showing an elaborate picture frame and perhaps a slightly damaged canvas.

Stencilling

Stencilling grew alongside the demand for patterned wallpapers, although it has its origins long before, when it was used to apply a repeat pattern or regular motif to the wall. The word probably originates from the French *estenceler* meaning to cover with stars – a very pretty image indeed.

From the late 18th century, stencilling was popular in areas where wallpapers were expensive. It gained much favour among the colonial pioneers, particularly the Pennsylvanian Dutch settlers whose patterns – the tulip is especially well known – are still used today. During the Gothic revival in Victorian times, stencilling heraldic devices was used extensively in churches.

To achieve the look of early stencilling, it is worth remembering that there was no degree of shading which can be achieved with modern paints today. Instead, colours appeared in solid blocks.

Where stencilling often imitated wallpaper patterns for those who could not afford the real thing, so many other techniques were developed for the same reason.

Faux effects

Marble – a heavy and expensive polished stone – was copied extensively in middle class Victorian homes, although the origins of this technique like so many others, are found in ancient Egypt.

Stone effects such as porphyry and granite were also popular. In the early 19th century they were achieved by spattering paint on to a solid ground or base. Later, sponging was more commonly employed to achieve a similar effect.

Likewise, bambooing was fashionable in the 18th and early 19th centuries as part of the chinoiserie craze. Bamboo was expensive and rare here, although cheap and abundant in the Orient; hence decorators sought to turn cheaper products into bamboo. Bamboo was even used as a wall finish. By the end of the 19th century though, the fashion had passed and so had the technique; only in recent years has it been revived.

Many of these beautiful effects have been preserved, sadly, many less notable establishments have been destroyed along with some interesting decoration.

I do wish I had seen the woodgrained panels in a large building close to my home. Demolished in the mid-1980s, this building was a hospital during the war. A gynaecologist, who is also an amateur architect, ardent historian and friend, on rescuing material before demolition remarked: 'For goodness sake break that panelling off the walls before they knock the building down!'

How many other locations boasting paint masterpieces have we lost? And how many more will we find?

Decorating standards

Technology has made rapid strides in the development of paint this century and particularly in the last 30 years. Now, a lot of decorating is done by the householder and because of speed, lack of imagination or skill, a coat or two of emulsion is all that is undertaken. It is a far cry from early 19th century decorating standards which prescribed six stages for the preparation and painting of new wood alone. Colour schemes were created by the clever use of top glazes over base coats to produce intense final colours.

With the revival of interest in these old time-consuming but thrilling techniques, it is worth, like William Morris to look to 'times past when design was flourishing...'

Below left: This distinguished billiard room boasts hand-painted walls.
Below right: A beautifully hand-painted ceiling dating from the nineteenth century.
Bottom: A section of restored marbling and stencilling.

Part Two
CONFIDENCE WITH COLOUR

Colour is an enormously powerful medium and a major consideration in modern home decorating. It is also an emotive and intensely personal subject – especially when it comes to interior decoration. Nevertheless, the successful use of colour is immensely satisfying; and because it is cheap and easily accessible, it is certainly a field worth exploring.

When approaching colour for the first time, it is important not to be put off by the clichés and 'rules' which both experts and books propound. Rather take colour theory as a guideline which can assist you in forming good colour sense. It may take time and some trial and error to reach your own goals, but the ensuing personal satisfaction will be worth it.

If you take inspiration from the world around, you will be surprised to see the finely balanced combinations it presents. Look at the way colours interact in nature; absorb the ever-present spectacle of colour and texture, and take your cue from there.

Shades of blues, green and aquamarine combine to create a stunning interior. The effect of the bold colours has been toned down in an unusual way by dribbling diluted black colour down the walls.

COLOUR IN THE HOME

Colour is the fastest, least expensive and most noticeable way of altering an interior. It is also the most exciting.

By changing a few cushions or rearranging pictures in different rooms on new backgrounds, it is possible to create a totally different atmosphere. By simply changing flowers, rugs or loose covers on furniture, seasonal changes are immediately achieved; thus enabling us to make our homes seem warmer in winter and cooler in summer.

Furthermore, almost anything which is visually pleasing can be converted into an interior scheme; and if the right shades and proportions of colour are used, you will be surprised to find that there are very few colours which do not go together.

Undoubtedly the success or failure of colour combinations does depend on other factors too: on pattern, texture, scale and proportion; on the location and lighting; the amount of each colour used; and the relationship of the colours chosen to each other. The use of broken colour, as achieved by using paint techniques, will also have a profound effect on the final result. Different techniques, too, can give interiors new dimensions.

While there must be balance within a house, the colours chosen should also suit the whole family. It is therefore imperative that colour likes and dislikes are ascertained before a scheme is decided upon and implemented.

Never blindly follow fashion or friends. Each colour has its own energy and it interacts differently with all other colours. Colours reinforce statements and send messages. They support interior design schemes and trigger reactions. Remember that individual preference will, to a large extent, determine what works: what is right for your neighbour may not be right for you.

The colour wheel is made up of twelve basic colours: the three pure primary colours, as well as three secondary and six tertiary colours.

THE THEORY OF COLOUR

Basic terminology relating to colour can be baffling to amateurs. This brief and simple introduction, which encompasses the broad implications of colour theory, is designed to minimise the threatening mystique which puts so many people off.

Colour is often the most memorable feature of an interior. Without doubt, the ability to use colours positively and beautifully is an admirable asset. This does not mean that colour has to be bold or bright. But it should give pleasure.

Next time you see a rainbow against a dark, dank, grey sky, try to extricate the colours and count how many hues there are. Then (if indeed you are a guilty party), wonder why you are stuck with porridge and muesli shades.

THE COLOUR WHEEL

The colour wheel, developed by Isaac Newton when he was studying the effects of a beam of light shining through a glass prism, is a great educational tool. Comprising 12 basic colours from which all identifiable hues are based, the colour wheel is a spectrum, like a rainbow, but joined at both ends.

Primary colours

Looking at the colour wheel, one identifies three primary colours: red, yellow and blue. These are colours in their strongest form and they cannot be produced by mixing other colours. They are spaced equidistant around the colour wheel and all colours are variations of them – mixed either with each other, or with black or white. These three colours are more intense or brilliant than secondary colours . . .

Secondary colours

If two primaries are mixed in equal parts, the resultant colours are called secondaries. This way we obtain green (a mixture of yellow and blue); orange (red and yellow); and violet (red and blue). These colours are more intense than tertiary colours . . .

Tertiary colours

If a primary colour is mixed with its closest secondary, a tertiary colour results. So we have six tertiaries: yellow-orange, red-orange, red-violet, yellow-green, blue-green and blue-violet.

THE PSYCHOLOGY OF COLOUR

There is no doubt that colour has an effect on people's emotions – although as individuals react so differently, any formal colour psychology is difficult to define. Sensitivity to colour may differ according to culture and upbringing, and it may also change with age and physical well-being. However, the psychological impulses we generally attribute to different colours are linked to primitive associations with nature. Although strong, vibrant colours may suggest splendour and joy; red can imply danger, like fire: it stimulates the brain and is exciting, but too much may make us restless. Blue is like ice: it is said to reduce excitability, but it is also mysterious and in excess may induce melancholia. Yellow is the sunshine colour: it is cheerful and draws attention. Green is associated with leaves and grass and growing plants: it is peaceful, cooling and may act as a sedative. When mellow, it may also be nostalgic. The ochres and browns are of the earth – warm, invigorating, cheerful and strong.

Non-colours

Technically, there are three true non-colours, black, white and grey (when it is mixed purely from black and white).

White When this non-colour is placed beside or between two colours, you see the true value of these colours. At the same time, white is a balanced mixture of each colour of the spectrum, and it can be used successfully as an accent. One colour plus white is a particularly easy and successful formula for interiors.

Black Often sombre and overpowering on its own, black is almost always used as an accent.

Grey A true neutral, colourless grey has little value in a colour scheme. It usually works best when used with texture and pattern. It is worth remembering that equal amounts of complementary colours always give grey.

WARM COLOURS AND COOL COLOURS

Colour can raise the temperature of a room visually, although a classification into warm and cool colours can be misleading.

Generally it is true that reds and yellows are warm, blues are cool and green mostly takes the middle of the road. However, there are warm blues, which contain red, and cool greens, which are produced with more blue than yellow. In addition, colours are affected by each other; so by placing a green near a lot of blue it could appear cooler than it would otherwise seem.

COLOUR AND TONE

Many people find it difficult to live with very deep or vivid colours, preferring to 'tone' them down a little. It takes practise to recognise tonal values though, and it is, therefore, not always easy to exploit fully the use of tone in colour.

While a hue is colour at full saturation, tone refers to how light or dark a colour is. So a hue is more intense than its tone; and as tones move further down their hue, they become less and less intense. Colours with the same tonal values also contain equal amounts of white or black: the addition of white resulting in a tint and the addition of black, in a shade.

TRANSPARENT COLOUR

For centuries, artists have used transparent glazes and diluted water colourwashes to create beautiful paintings. But it comes as some surprise to realise that similar transparent paint glazes have been utilised by decorators, since John Fowler popularised their use in the 1930s.

Instead of applying solid colour which will effectively eliminate your background, transparent colour – applied in successive layers – allows light to reflect the base below, adding depth and character.

BROKEN COLOUR

While there is no doubt that plain, honest, solid colour has an important place in decorating, the discovery of broken colour techniques opens up a whole new world.

The effects range from subtle shading and dappled backdrops to vivid, textured surfaces. Glazes and washes are applied or removed in a manner which achieves a wide variety of broken finishes.

COLOUR CHANGES

All colours change according to the way in which they are used.

Juxtaposition When colours are placed next to each other, the intensity and effect may change. No one colour exists in isolation and colour interactions inevitably produce harmonious or discordant effects. Although not always practically possible, separating the colours with a non-colour can solve this problem.

Texture Different surfaces of the same colour will appear to differ, as the rougher the surface, the more colour it will absorb. Take two identically coloured fabrics like smooth silk and coarse, textured wool and you will see the difference immediately. Matt and gloss paints, as well as broken paint finishes, follow the same pattern.

Light Colours get their true value from clear, bright, natural light. Dim light tends to neutralise colour, while artificial and reflected light alters it. Incandescent light usually gives a yellowish cast, while fluorescents make colours blue. When choosing colour the form of natural or artificial lighting used must be taken into account.

Black is a positive accent in a neutral room where non-colours are in evidence.

COLOUR SCHEMES

Successful colour schemes depend on inspiration and emotion as much as knowledge. Colour theory should be accompanied by experimentation. Experience colour: mix it yourself; explore its various combinations; and most of all, enjoy it.

When choosing a colour scheme, it is essential for it to relate to the specific room: enhancing its purpose and function, as well as creating mood and atmosphere.

Although it is generally best to allow one colour to dominate, the eye can handle as many as three colours in a basic scheme. Each space makes its own demands so think of a series of colour schemes which work in your house as a whole. This is especially important when you can see from room to room.

Types of colour schemes

There are various types of definable colour schemes which use the colour wheel as a base. In general these may be either harmonious or contrasting.

Monochromatic These harmonious schemes rely on one hue being used with variations of intensity, texture and pattern. This non-aggressive approach can be sophisticated, but it can also be dull.

Analogous These harmonious schemes include three or four colours which are adjacent on the colour wheel. Warm or cool colours can be used, but to succeed, one hue should dominate.

Complementary These contrasting schemes rely on two colours from opposite sides of the colour wheel. One colour should predominate while the second becomes an accent.

Triadic These contrasting schemes are difficult to carry off and are best when used in conjunction with a lot of white. Here any three colours equidistant from one another may be included.

From an ordinary look with wallpaper to rich Persian colours created with paint.

Choosing a colour scheme

Economic factors make it sensible to choose furnishings and fittings before choosing the colours which will complement or set them off. If you are aiming for constant change and colour excitement, this can be limiting; in which case, it will help to opt for neutral furnishings so you can change wall colours and accessories frequently, at relatively low cost.

A dynamic colour transformation.

Of course personal preference will play a major role in your choice of colour, but there are several basic factors that should also be taken into account.

Aspect If a room gets lots of sun and is very warm, the obvious solution is to choose a cool colour. However, if this seems a bit drastic, a successful compromise is to add a little blue to a warm colour, thus 'cooling' it a little.

Size Strong, warm colours appear to advance, making a room seem smaller and more intimate. Conversely, whites, neutrals, pastel tints and the cool colours are not easily defined by the eye so they appear to recede. So the lighter the value of a pale, cool colour the larger (and colder) a room will appear.

Function Bold colours tend to stimulate conversation and can therefore work well in living rooms, but might create insomnia in a bedroom. Generally, pale, soft tones are most successful in bedrooms although primary colours work for children. In dining rooms and entrance halls you can safely be more dramatic with colour, as these areas are not in constant use.

MIXING COLOUR

These days it is possible to buy almost any colour ready mixed, but often only in relatively large quantities. Many decorative paint finishes require surprisingly small quantities of paint, so it is often worth mixing your own.

If you have never had experience mixing colour – either in the art field or for interior decoration – it is wise to start with small quantities and to keep careful notes of all proportions and colours used. There is nothing more frustrating than creating a wonderful finish which even you cannot reproduce.

Achieving a chosen colour effect may be a difficult, even bewildering process, for those who have never mixed paint before. So before you start, try to work out logically which colours you need. Do not add tints haphazardly or you could end up with a muddy sludge. Instead, try to limit your mixture to two or three colours.

You are going to need a basic palette and your choice will obviously rely on the colour schemes you have chosen. Just remember that having too many colours to play with can be confusing and may have displeasing results.

Colour source

There are several ways to colour paint and, as long as the mediums used are compatible, ingredients may be mixed. (For further information on paints and colourants see pages 88–89).

Raw pigments The most commonly available powder pigments are yellow ochre, red iron oxide, green oxide and black oxide, all of which can be used to achieve wonderful natural effects. These are only available from specialist suppliers.

Tinters Universal tinters are used commercially to colour paint. The advantage of this form of colourant is its variety and compatibility with both water and oil-based paints. Although all paint companies have slightly different combinations, most rely on 12 tinters including black, white, various reds, yellows, orange, green, blue and violet. Some hardware stores will readily sell small quantities (which is all you will need) of tinter from their mixing machines. However, most good decorating suppliers sell a wide selection of tinters in small tubes.

Oil colours Artists' oils are a wonderful source of colour and a huge range is available from several manufacturers. Art shops and good stationery suppliers will sell them.

Acrylic colours Artists' acrylics may be successfully used to mix with emulsions. As with artists' oils, colours are numerous. Generally, acrylics come in large, fat tubes and are sold in art shops or stationers.

The basic palette

Successful mixing of colour is a skill which improves with practice. The idea is to develop a feel for colour rather than to rely on theory. Start with a limited range of colours, adding to your basic palette as your confidence increases.

You can work with primary colours, but the mixed colours (oils, acrylics and water paints prepared for artists) – crimson reds (like rose madder, vermilion and alizarin crimson), blues (including cool Prussian blue and the warmer French ultramarine), yellows (like cadmium) and greens (like viridian and translucent terre-verte) – produce particularly good colours. 'Dirty' earthy colours – yellow ochre, the oxides, both raw and burnt sienna, as well as raw and burnt umber – are also invaluable for adding depth and warmth.

Altering colour

Having mixed a colour, you may find it is not quite what you wanted. While experimentation and experience are the keys to success, a few stock solutions can help.

Lightening colours The addition of white is the obvious solution, although it may also change the colour. If this happens, another hue can be added to give it a boost, while a complementary colour can soften without altering tone.

Darkening colours It is always simpler to lighten a colour than to darken it – and it is terribly easy to create muddy browns and greys. If the colour you have mixed is too light, try adding a little more of the dominant colours you are working with. It is probably best to avoid black or the vitality of the original hue may be destroyed. However black artists' paints do vary and ivory black can be useful.

Brightening colours The answer is usually to experiment. Although white may work with some yellows, if there is any red in the yellow, it will become dull.

Subduing colours Most colours can be quickly and easily subdued. Look for a related hue in a less intense form.

A splash of colour can brighten any room, as these exciting colour combinations show. Without colour these rooms would have been plain and ordinary.

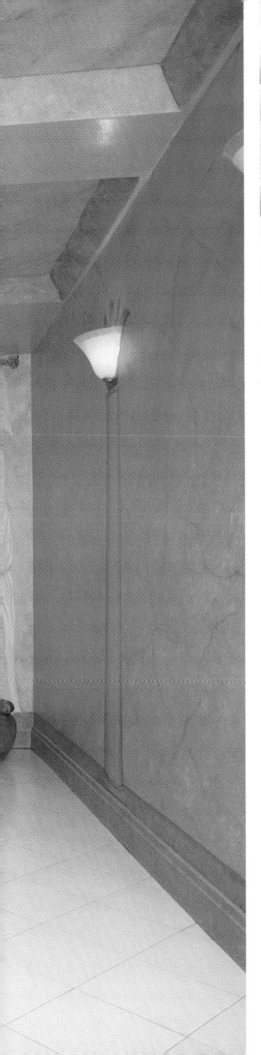

Part Three
DECORATIVE PAINT TECHNIQUES

The discovery of decorative paint techniques, old and new, is exciting and exhilarating. Within this world of painted warmth, of washes and wonderful glazes; of fake fantasies and fabulous finishes, there are all the ingredients for successful interior design. It is rather like opening an enormous paintbox of colour, pattern and texture . . . although there is no doubt that it can be intimidating when it is new. You do not know how to tackle the new-found techniques, where to use them or even if you want to use them at all.

The beauty of decorative paint finishes is that they are generally inexpensive, easy to apply and easy to eradicate if they fail or when you tire of them. By using washes and manipulating oil-based glazes, you can achieve a variety of textures and effects which will revitalise the most tired and dreary of rooms.

Many of the standard finishes are reminiscent of wallpapers or fabrics like hessian, crushed cotton, velvet, satin or silk. Others produce effects more like natural materials: marble, granite, malachite or stone.

We hope that the pictures we present, together with the accompanying guidelines, will give you the courage and conviction that these decorative paint treatments have a place in your home too.

This magnificent entrance hall with a difference was created with clever trompe l'oeil and a combination of other techniques, including marbling.

MODERN PAINT TECHNIQUES

Starting with sponging, stippling and ragging on, the techniques we use today can be disarmingly simple. But, at the same time, as the professionals prove, these may be compounded with others to create amazingly sophisticated finishes. It does not matter whether you want an ordinarily attractive surface, a gloriously distinguished coating or a subtle, time-weathered patina, decorative paint techniques can do it all.

We have included most of the simpler techniques in the sections which follow, providing step-by-step instructions for those we have found to be most popular. You can quickly learn the basics of sponging, ragging, rag rolling, dragging, colourwashing, marbling and stencilling and then gain inspiration from the photographs which show just what can be achieved in real situations.

But look carefully. Often the effects are so subtle and subdued, it is difficult to pinpoint what gives a room its warmth, romance or vitality. Soft sponging may add a dappled, sun-splashed quality; strong dragging suggest an elegant air; while rag rolling in a deep colour might add gracious sophistication. These techniques, differently applied, will have quite another effect.

The weathered effect of several layers of glaze rubbed onto the walls (above), contrasts with a subtle effect achieved by ragging on (below).

SPECIALIST TECHNIQUES

To ensure that we portray a true cross-section of skills and finishes, we have photographed rooms painted by professionals as well as interiors tackled by enthusiastic amateurs.

We have deliberately excluded specialist techniques like gilding, and have only touched on furniture antiquing and liming.

While there are vague rumblings of discontent from a handful of professional decorators and painters who disapprove of the sudden amateur interest and activity in this fascinating field, mostly there is enthusiasm and an eagerness to share ideas. At the same time, a few purists insist that substitute materials and cheaper equipment lowers standards to such an extent to make nonsense of techniques like marbling and woodgraining. They insist that certain items – like badger and dragging brushes – are indispensable. During the past year we have explored so many homes and seen so many lovely finishes created with home-made mixtures and 'wrong' brushes that we know this is not entirely true.

You do not have to strive for perfection to achieve a finish you will be proud of.

Materials and equipment

The paint industry is a sophisticated and ever-changing technological world. For this reason we have focused on many of our own tried and tested recipes for washes and glazes. All rely on easily available products. However, commercial scumble glazes, often based on traditional and secret compounds, are frequently used, thinned with turpentine or white spirit, in preference to home-made linseed oil glazes which take longer to dry.

Perhaps the best-known glaze is Ratcliffe's transparent oil glaze manufactured for many years in Britain. Emulsion glazes – like Ratcliffe's emulsion glazecoat – are sometimes used for techniques; although their primary use is as a water-based sealer.

Other popular makes include Craig and Rose who manufacture both a varnish and an oil-based scumble glaze called Glaze Clear.

Commercial oil-based scumble glazes may be used in place of any of the oil-based recipes we recommend (see a selection of recipes on page 91).

When it comes to equipment, it is true that traditional techniques often call for traditional tools. But for the average home decorator, specialist equipment like woodgraining combs and heart-grainers, pencil overgrainers, stiff-bristled stippling brushes and soft badger brushes are not vital to achieve a good effect. Therefore, we have suggested suitable substitutes wherever possible. The traditional tools have not, however, been ignored.

Equipment and materials range from specialist tools to inexpensive home-made glazes and household items like the black plastic bags used in this room.

SPONGING

Sponging is technically the simplest paint technique of all. It is commonly used on wall surfaces, but it is also a successful medium for furniture and woodwork.

The simplicity of sponging, thought to have its origins in folk art, makes it a popular technique with amateurs. However, to be really successful, it does require a sensitive touch.

It is possible to create varied effects, ranging from a soft, subtle finish to one which is crisp and colourful. The trick, however, is to avoid the impression of spots of paint simply dabbed onto the surface. Badly done, sponging looks like ugly splodges of paint which is enough to put anyone off the technique.

Each of the pastel colours in the curtaining was colour-matched, mixed in emulsion and then sponged onto the wall to echo the fabric.

You can sponge on or off (if you are using an oil-based or scumble glaze), depending on the effects you want to achieve. Generally it is easier to sponge on, although sponging off will result in a more mellow, dappled look. If you are using more than one colour, you will obviously have to sponge on – at least from the second colour. Always bear in mind that your final colour will tend to predominate.

While large surface areas like walls look particularly attractive when sponged, this technique is also suitable for decorating furniture. Wooden chairs, for instance, may be sponged in several colours to match the upholstery. Small items like boxes or picture frames may also be sponged.

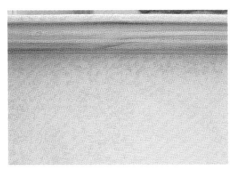

Paint

Sponging is one technique which is quick, easy and effective with an emulsion (water-based) paint, although some people prefer to stick with oil-based glazes.

Emulsions It is quite acceptable to use an ordinary matt emulsion for sponging on, although a silk emulsion or mid-sheen acrylic paint will give you a nice lustre. Use the paint as it is, or dilute it 2:1 with water. The addition of an acrylic sealer will add luminosity.

Oil-based paints Another simple option for sponging on is oil-based eggshell or satin-wood paint, diluted with turpentine or white spirit in a ratio of about 2:1 (paint:solvent). It is easy to work with and is especially useful for decorating small items of furniture and woodwork.

Glazes Oil-based glazes are useful for sponging off as the addition of linseed oil helps to keep the surface wet and workable. Even a very small quantity – say half the amount of oil:solvent – will make a difference. To prevent excessive discoloration, especially when using pastel colours, use purified linseed oil or artists' refined linseed oil. If you do not want to mix your own glaze, use a commercial scumble glaze mixed with an oil-based eggshell and turpentine in equal parts.

Base paints An unusual option is the transparent or translucent paint base – available for mixing deep emulsion and gloss colours in a paint shop mixing machine. These can be stained with universal tinters.

Top: The effect of a translucent, shiny glaze over flat emulsion looks quite different to a more regular sponging (top), where pink and cream over white give a soft, subdued feel to a feminine room.
Above, centre and above left: Subtle shades simply give texture to a living room wall.
Above right: Stencils border a simple sponged wall, adding character and style.

Above, right and below left: an ordinary living room is transformed by sponging deep red over a khaki-coloured ground.
Below centre: A translucent glaze sponged over emulsion gives this bedroom a warm glow.
Below right: Subtle sponging in yellow adds texture, depth and vitality.
Bottom: Stencils on a sponged wall.

Preparation

Your surface must be clean and sound before painting begins (see pages 72–73). Sponging relies on broken colour for its success so particular care must be taken with your base coat (ground) colour. You can use contrasting colours, but it is wise to stick to similar tones and good, fresh combinations. Standard paints may be purchased in the required colour or you can tint your own (see page 89).

Tools

The only special equipment you will need is a reasonable-sized marine sponge (the bigger the better if you are working on a wall, although the bigger the holes, the less discreet the effect will be). This must be wet with water and then wrung out so it expands and softens before work begins. Avoid synthetic sponges as they produce a regular, rather blotchy, hard-edged effect.

Technique

When applying the paint or glaze onto your surface, it is important not to overload the sponge or you will get runs, drips and thick coagulations of colour. You want to see the textured print the sponge leaves, so make sure it is damp rather than sodden with paint.

When you squeeze paint out of the sponge, do not squeeze it into the paint you are working with as you could get bubbles which will make it difficult to use. Instead of dipping the sponge into the paint, apply the paint sparingly onto the sponge with a brush. Or, if you are using an oil-based glaze, satin gloss or eggshell paint, brush a small quantity onto a piece of hardboard and use it as a palette, dabbing your sponge over the liquid. Before attacking your surface, it is a good idea to blot the sponge a few times on a clean section of the hardboard or on paper. Avoid newspaper as the black print tends to come off with the paint.

It is possible to sponge on any number of colours and two or three shades chosen to match curtains or upholstery can be par-

ticularly effective. The results are usually more successful if the colours used are similar in tone, although extreme contrasts like powder blue over dusky pink or even black over white can work.

Sponge the entire surface with one colour before embarking on the next; and make sure it is completely dry or you might get a cloudy mess or stippled finish. As you sponge, constantly change the position of your wrist to avoid regular lines and repetitive patterns.

If you are working with more than two colours, leave plenty of background colour each time, building up the effect by gradually overlapping the colours.

When sponging off (sometimes called sponge stippling), it is necessary to clean the sponge regularly – remembering to squeeze the solvent out thoroughly each time. Do not try and sponge off an emulsion paint or wash. It will simply dry much too fast.

Finally, it is a good idea to 'tidy' a dappled, sponged surface with a band of solid colour or even a wallpaper border.

A large marine sponge has been used to apply colour above the picture rail for a granite-like effect. Solid colour below the rail matches rich-coloured drapes.

1. Gently sponge on the first colour.

2. Change your wrist movement.

3. When dry, dab on a second shade.

4. The final colour will predominate.

DECORATIVE PAINT TECHNIQUES   **29**

RAGGING AND RAG ROLLING

Ragging and rag rolling are well-known and commonly used techniques which are quick, easy and versatile. It is possible to achieve an amazingly varied array of effects depending on the material used.

A multitude of finishes can be created with a general 'family' of fashionable techniques which utilise rags and cloths of various kinds.

Lumped together vaguely as 'ragged finishes' they include ragging on and ragging off; rag rolling on and rag rolling off; bagging or plastic-bag stippling; and even a version I have seen referred to as 'mutton clothing'. The results which can be achieved are vast and varied, depending on the material used to rag; the consistency of the glaze

An elegant entrance hall owes its success as much to simplicity as to a stylish use of paint finishes, with ragged walls matching large terracotta floor tiles.

you are ragging over (or ragging off); and the way this glaze is manipulated.

Simply dabbing a glaze with a bunched-up rag, bag or mutton cloth will give three different impressions. Similarly, rag rolling with sausages of cotton, stockinette or linen will also give totally different finishes.

Although there is little doubt that the basics of ragging are the simplest in this category, the effects of rag rolling (on or off) are more impressive, resulting in more sophisticated finishes. Well done, rag rolling can create the effect of soft velvet, crumpled cotton or crushed silk.

The best way is to experiment on a board (tedious as this may seem); or to play around on an inconspicuous area of wall. If you are

working with a glaze containing linseed oil, it is going to take a while to dry thoroughly, so you will be able to wipe it clean if you hate the effect.

If you are aiming for a ragged-off finish and want to be really efficient, work with a friend. One can paint the glaze onto the prepared base – in a chequerboard pattern – and the other can rag or rag roll it off. Alternatively work on relatively small areas at a time and make sure the edges do not dry out or you will have nasty lines in the finished product.

Glaze

The use of a glaze is fundamental to the success of both ragging and rag rolling. To rag off, it is essential that an oil-based glaze is used; but to rag on, a water-based glaze makes an acceptable substitute. You can use a proprietary scumble glaze – mixed with eggshell, tinted for colour and thinned with turpentine or white spirit – although it is surprisingly easy to mix your own (see page 91).

Preparation

Basic surface preparation is, as always, essential. The surface must be clean, sound and should be painted with the appropriate base coat. Both an oil-based satin or eggshell finish (for oil-based glazes) and a vinyl silk emulsion (for water-based glazes) give a good, smooth surface for rag rolling.

Colour

The colour of your base coat is important as the effects achieved rely partly on the relation of ground colour to glaze. It is a good idea to use colours which are tonally similar, although strong contrast can sometimes work.

In general, closely related colour helps soften the image; crimson reds and burnt sienna, as well as browns and even black, will help achieve a leather look; while deep reds and greys can create the idea of soft velvet.

Combined Materials

Mix your glaze, choose your rags ... and you are ready to go.

Glaze mix There are numerous mixtures which are suitable for ragged finishes, and the choice will be largely personal. Try a glaze with a particularly high linseed oil content (see page 91). The linseed oil makes the glaze malleable and easy to work with. Although some professionals have criticised the recipe because of this, I have tested several others and still find this one to be the best.

The recipe is basically a 2:2:1 mix (paint:boiled linseed oil:turpentine), but making it up is a bit like cooking. The more you work with it, the more you will develop a feel for the correct consistency. Use a good-quality oil-based eggshell paint coloured with universal tinters or try the transparent base used for deep-shaded paints (see page 27). This is a particularly successful paint base for a ragging glaze.

Above left: Purple emulsion ragged onto a white wall surface gives textured colour to an interesting art deco-style living room. Above: Blue emulsion paint ragged over a yellow base gives these dining-room walls a special zest and sparkle.

Stained with universal tinters or artists' oil colours, it has a translucency which is hard to beat.

While some people simply dilute paint with water 2:1, a water-based glaze made with matt emulsion, water and silk emulsion or acrylic varnish mixed 2:2:1 is a more satisfactory emulsion glaze for ragged-on finishes. However, it is not as flexible as an oil-based glaze and does not have the same lustre.

Rags Before you start, decide on the effect you want and choose your rags accordingly. Some of the most commonly used materials are cotton (old sheets are perfect), mutton cloth or stockinette and crumpled, plastic bags. Coarse hessian will add a woven texture; vilene will give a crisp edge; and chamois leather, although expensive, gives a good, strong print. Just make sure your rags are lint-free or you will have unwanted texture sticking to your walls!

When ragging off, rags quickly become saturated with glaze and must be frequently swopped for clean ones. Instead of discarding, it is possible to soak them in turpentine and then wash for reuse.

Below: Both walls and ceiling of this large elegant drawing room are ragged.
Right: Subtle rag rolling off is trimmed by a black marbled skirting.
Below centre: Ragging can camouflage ugly features and create atmosphere.
Bottom: The related techniques of rag rolling off (left) and ragging on (right) can add character to even the most mundane domestic interiors.

Technique

The origins of ragging can be found in the annals of fine art under the general heading 'scumbling'. For this is, in essence, the same technique which artists have used for centuries to break up paint surfaces and achieve texture: dabbing and stippling their paintings to reveal images and colour beneath.

The application of this technique, in combination with the different materials chosen, determines the effect you will achieve.

RAGGING ON

This is probably the simplest version of a ragged technique, and rather like sponging on, but with fabric. The rag is dipped into glaze, thoroughly squeezed out, formed into a creased bundle and then dabbed onto the surface. Be sure to keep changing your wrist movement to achieve a varied and irregular pattern.

RAGGING OFF

Not as messy as ragging on, ragging off creates a softer, more flowing pattern. Here the bunched-up rags are pressed into glaze which has been painted onto the surface. Use a firm, dabbing movement to remove just enough glaze to leave a distinct impression. Wring your rag out when it becomes saturated with glaze. If this is not effective, discard it and use a new one.

Paint from top to bottom, in workable sections, always ensuring a wet edge. This is particularly important if you are working alone.

Two vastly different interiors (a bathroom and a study) illustrate how bold use of colour often benefits from the addition of a decorative paint technique like ragging – in any one of its varied forms.

RAGGING OFF

1. Paint glaze on to the wall surface.

2. Take a bunched-up rag and dab.

3. Continue doing this all over.

4. The effect achieved with cotton.

RAG ROLLING ON

1. Start with a sausage of rag.

2. Roll it gently over the surface.

3. Vary your direction to cover.

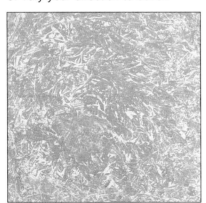

4. The effect should be crisp.

RAG ROLLING OFF

1. Paint a glaze on to the surface.

2. Roll a rag through the wet glaze.

3. The yellow ground shows through.

Colours and techniques have a definite effect on rooms which have been ragged and rag rolled. They vary from absolute subtlety in the softly rag-rolled rooms (right top and right centre) to the boldly hued study (right) and the more distinct patterns achieved in the dining room (opposite, bottom left).
Opposite: Plastic bags of various kinds can be used to achieve wonderful effects. Ordinary supermarket bags were used in the entrance hall (top) while black rubbish bags were used on the walls of the drawing room (bottom right).

RAG ROLLING ON

The effects of ragging on and rag rolling on are very different, the latter creating a more distinctive pattern. Once your rag has been dipped into the glaze mixture and squeezed out, it must be formed (but not folded) into a loose sausage which is literally rolled across the surface. Vary your direction to avoid distinct lines forming. Take care that the rags are consistently damp or you may find blotches occurring on the surface.

RAG ROLLING OFF

Rag rolling off gives the most dramatically beautiful effects of all, and even the slightest contrasts in tone achieve striking results. It works best on walls although it can be successful on smaller surfaces. Although not necessary, the effect can be softened by gently stippling the glaze before rolling off. The technique is a combination of ragging off and rag rolling on, using a bunched-up sausage of fabric to remove the glaze.

PLASTIC BAGGING

The non-absorbency of crackly plastic contributes to the deliciously crisp effect this offshoot of the ragged techniques achieves. The steps followed are exactly the same as ordinary ragging off, although the build-up of glaze is greater. Collect a bundle of old shopping bags and change them frequently, wiping the bag between dabs.

Black, plastic rubbish bags may also be used, but the effect will be softer and more mottled, like parchment.

PLASTIC BAG STIPPLING

1. Roughly paint on a glaze.

2. Bunch up a plastic shopping bag.

3. Firmly apply pressure for . . .

4. . . . . a gently uneven stippled finish.

DISTRESSING

Distressing is a form of antiquing and is used to simulate the effects of wear and tear on a newly painted surface.

Although all so-called broken colour may be called 'distressed', as a decorative paint technique distressing refers to the method of making new paint work appear naturally worn and graciously aged.

While a wall surface can be made to look faded by sensitive colourwashing, or darkened by subtle rubbing, the weather-beaten look of age requires something more. This does not mean to say that a distressed surface should look as though it is actually falling to pieces or that it should be grubby; instead it should add textured character and charm to a room.

A distressed wall in an elegant room adds charm. The painted trellis design further enhances the soft fabric-like finish this technique achieves.

Colour is of some importance in this technique. Basically, bright vivid colours are perceived as new; old means faded, washed out and pale. Sir John Fowler, the renowned English decorator, relied on soft colours and subtle shades to blend old and new. Some of the most enchanting examples of distressed wall surfaces are achieved using cool colours. Combinations like duck egg blue and mauve or pale lilac work well. However, that does not mean you can not use strong colours: warm earth colours such as terracotta and peach are effective.

Do not worry if distressing highlights imperfections. Professionals often deliberately aim to achieve this, making lumps and bumps into features.

Left: A classical look in a modern setting has been achieved with an attractive distressed finish in two contrasting colours. Fake stonework adds to the impact of the finish.
Below: A particularly attractive effect has been achieved by distressing the bold stencilling around a doorway.
Bottom: An eclectic styled interior is enhanced by the introduction of water distressing down the painted brick walls.

Technique

The irony of this kind of distressed effect is that people could so easily stumble upon it by accident, trying to rectify or improve a finish they do not like, or have tired of.

Basically, thick colour is first painted onto the wall and then, when dry, sanded off, leaving highlights and shadows where underneath imperfections would be found. Alternatively, a wire brush or even a scourer (on smaller surfaces) may be used.

Although it works best on uneven surfaces, a very rough wall can be problematic as you will not be able to sand too much away without getting down to bare plaster on the tips of all the little bumps.

A totally smooth wall could first be painted with a white or pastel, textured coating to provide a rough vehicle for later sanding. It will, however, lack those natural imperfections which add such interesting character.

Effect

The final effects achieved depend largely on the amount of colour removed by sanding your wall. Perhaps inevitably, the effect of this sanding also smooths the wall surface, so you will have a texture effect which has a satiny feel and perfect finish for stencilling.

DRAGGING

Dragging is a formal finish which has its origins in rudimentary woodgraining techniques. Well done, it creates a softly striped effect which can look beautifully elegant.

Dragging is a demanding technique which requires patience, tenacity and a steady hand. Although it was used as a basic technique in the mid-eighteenth century when woodgraining was done extensively throughout the world, it was distinguished 1930s decorator, John Fowler, who popularised it in its own right, as a decorative paint finish.

Beautiful, long-haired, dragging brushes – now made from hog's hair, horsehair or pure bristle – were the traditional tools and are still used by some professional painters.

Defying the rules, this attractive bedroom was cloth dragged with an acrylic paint, to complement both the design and colour in the fabric.

However, they are difficult to buy and outrageously expensive. Instead, any coarse, relatively long-haired paintbrush will do. Try using a good-quality, bristle block brush on walls and an ordinary household paintbrush for woodwork and other small surfaces. Surprisingly, a sponge and cloth may also be used with great success.

Although dragging can be wonderfully effective on walls, the amateur painter should start with smaller surface areas. If you are determined to drag an entire wall, it helps (in fact, some say it is essential) to have a partner. A good compromise is to drag below a dado rail (which could be stencilled or masked in if there is not a moulded rail), and rag, wash or sponge

Preparation

An evenly dragged finish cannot be achieved unless the surface is completely smooth and sound. All cracks should be filled, and sanded when dry. Paint with universal undercoat before applying the base coat. If the plaster finish itself is rough, dragging should be avoided.

Assuming you have prepared the surface thoroughly, you should not have a problem ensuring that the base coat (ground) has a good, smooth, even finish. Here it is preferable to use an eggshell or satin finish of the appropriate hue.

Left: Dragged faux panels in a pretty pink pastel-shaded dining room.
Below: Dragging below a stencilled dado.
Bottom: Dragged panels combine beautifully with striped wallpaper.

above it. Dragging is also a particularly successful finish for woodwork – especially doors, frames and skirtings – and for pieces of furniture.

Whatever your surface, for dragging to be elegantly effective, it is important to have just the right colour contrast between your base coat and dragging glaze. Our dragging board (see page 40) shows four effects crated with two base colours and two glazes. Experiment on your own board before you start work.

Glaze

To achieve beautifully fine stripes of colour, like loosely woven cloth, it is important to keep a wet edge while dragging. For this reason it is often best to work with a glaze containing a substantial amount of linseed oil. The 2:2:1 scumble glaze recipe (paint:boiled linseed oil:turpentine) works particularly well (see page 91). However, I have sponge dragged a narrow wall area successfully with a totally linseed-free mix, using an oil-based eggshell diluted 2:1 with pure turpentine oil.

Do not try to drag with a water-based glaze. It simply dries too fast to be visually effective.

Dragging is a suitable finish for both walls and woodwork like doors.
Top: The technique adds distinction to a formal dining-room situation.
Above: Dragging complements ragging.

Technique

The biggest bugbear of dragging is the need for a good, straight movement from top to bottom. If you are not very careful you will encounter problems.

Straight lines With walls, problem number one is ensuring that your brush strokes are straight. A good aid is a plumb line, used several times along the wall. Be warned that if you have got a very high ceiling, it will be doubly difficult.

Joins With walls, especially high ones, it will be virtually impossible to drag from top to bottom in one movement without wavering as you climb up and down a ladder. Ideally, areas to be dragged should only be as long as one's stretch. If you are forced to break the dragging movement, do so at variable intervals as you work. This way you can avoid a definite line of conspicuous joins. By feathering your second stroke slightly, where the two sections meet, you can subtly blend them together.

DRAGGING (on a two-tone board)

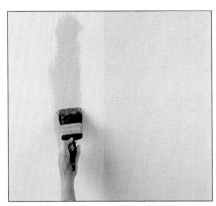

1. Begin painting on the glaze.

5. Notice the effects of each ground.

2. Cover a manageable surface area.

6. Achieve subtle changes this way.

3. Firmly drag a brush through the glaze.

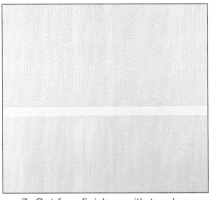

7. Get four finishes with two bases.

4. Take care to maintain a wet edge.

Wet edge The importance of maintaining a wet edge cannot be over-emphasised when it comes to dragging. Once your glaze begins to dry, you will get a quick build-up of colour. The most satisfactory way of overcoming this problem is to work with a partner, one applying the glaze and the other dragging it off before the edges become tacky and unmalleable. If you are forced to work on your own, work fast and do not stop until you have completed a definable surface. Stop at the corner of a room, but not in the centre of a wall.

Dragged walls frame a beautiful real marble fireplace (right top), and provide a sophisticated backdrop (right bottom).

Tidy ends Dragging is used surprisingly infrequently on walls, partly because it is a fiddly business cleaning at the top and bottom – where the drag begins and ends. If this is not done, these areas inevitably look irregular and messy, totally destroying that wonderful look of elegance and sophistication dragging creates. One tip is to start each drag pushing your brush up slightly before dragging downwards. Alternatively, neaten the edge by wiping it with a cloth-covered finger.

A fail-safe answer for amateurs is to add a solid band of colour (or even a wallpaper border), top and bottom, once the glaze has dried. In the right situation, it can save the day.

Painting
Paint your glaze on in manageable sections (about 30 cm/12 in wide bands – and not more than two or three widths of your dragging tool), working from top to bottom.

Return to the top end of your surface and, with firm, even pressure, steadily drag the brush (or substitute) through the glaze. If the strips are too cloudy, you usually drag through the glaze a second time. Just remember that you are removing colour every time you repeat this process. As you work, wipe your brush regularly with a clean cloth to prevent a build-up of glaze, otherwise the final impressions will be cloudy and indistinct.

COLOURWASHING

Colourwashing produces a charming, un-pretentious and lively translucent finish which is particularly well suited to cottage-style or rustic country homes. Of all the decorative paint finishes, colourwashing is the most fresh and natural. It creates a wonderful, weathered look of dappled sunlight and faded cotton, reminiscent of country cottages and rambling farmhouses.

With colourwashing, it is possible to simulate the lovely unrefined effects which cannot be created with solid paint colour. It is especially effective when walls are rough and uneven and makes a particularly suitable background for stencilling. Furthermore, it is the cheapest finish of all and it is not difficult to master. In fact,

This brushy finish (above) contrasts with a simple country look achieved by washing the walls with a rose-hued paint diluted 4:1 with water (below).

colourwashing was the first decorative paint finish I tackled, and in a single day, I transformed my lounge using a single litre of paint diluted with water.

Traditionally colourwashing was done with distemper – a chalky product usually containing whiting. Although a very old-fashioned medium, distemper is coming back into vogue among interior decorators. Colour-washing using this technique is once again growing in popularity, with thinned distemper being used over a distempered background. In fact, distemper is now available in a range of colours. Modern paint cannot be applied over distemper or limewash though and it is quite difficult to remove (see pages 74–75).

These walls were washed with diluted emulsion to which an acrylic sealer was added. Four successive coats were applied to build up the glowing pink colour.

Paint

There are various ways to mix a wash, depending on the paint or colour medium you choose.

Distemper Although outdated, distemper (traditionally a mixture of whiting and starch) is growing again in demand. It is cheap, but creates major problems when it comes to overcoating as the dusty, chalky surface prevents adhesion of subsequent paints. It is not recommended unless you are working on a previously distempered surface, in which case you will need to add pigment powder to your wash or buy a pre-coloured distemper.

Whitewash An exterior coating made from lime and fat, whitewash (or limewash) has the same chalky drawbacks as distemper.

Emulsion A good-quality low-sheen emulsion is ideal for a wash. It can be diluted with water in any ratio from about 1:4 to 1:10, although an extreme dilution will result in what paint manufacturers will identify as a hopelessly underbound mixture. This means, in turn, that the scrubability of the finish will be minimised. The solution is to protect your surface with an acrylic varnish or sealer once the wash has thoroughly dried. Avoid polyurethane as it yellows and will alter the colour.

Raw pigment Pigment powder – like yellow ochre, red iron oxide and green chrome oxide – as well as universal tinters can be added to water to make a wash. Very little powder is needed and it must be thoroughly mixed. It is a runny and messy wash, and powder pigments are difficult to obtain, but the result is wonderfully translucent. The addition of a little emulsion paint will help bind the mixture, but also increase opacity.

Artists' gouache This form of water-based paint commonly used in commercial and graphic design, works well in a wash as its opaque colour is intensely brilliant. Add to a little white emulsion before diluting. Protect with an acrylic sealer to increase lightfastness.

Glaze If you want to colourwash with an oil-based mixture, dilute eggshell with turpentine. The same guidelines as for emulsion apply. As this is a somewhat messy process – and oil-based paints are more difficult to clean than emulsion – I prefer to rub on oil-based glazes (to which linseed oil has been added) for a similar finish.

However, colourwashing can be done successfully with modern emulsion paints, raw pigments in water or mixtures containing artists' colour to create a wash. Although water-based washes have a freshness which oils cannot match, it is also possible to use an oil-based glaze to achieve a colourwashed look.

Washes

The basic concept of a wash is to apply watery colour to the wall, adding depth and character. The dilution of your mixture, the colour medium added and the number of coats applied will all affect the finish.

Preparation

While basic preparation is the same as for any wall surface, the importance of a good, sound base for colourwashing cannot be overemphasised. Its translucency draws attention to a badly prepared base coat, highlighting any defects and dirt. Interior filler will show unless it is coated with universal undercoat prior to painting, as it is chalky and porous and absorbs more colour than the surrounding painted surface. At the end of the day, minor defects often add character to the finish, but dirty marks look sloppy.

Colourwashing is particularly effective with soft, mellow, pretty colours as well as rich, earthy tones and warm ochres. It often looks best over a pristine white base which adds to its luminosity.

Although for permanence it is a good idea to seal colourwashed surfaces, there is also something to be said for allowing the surface to gently mellow with wear. After all, traditionally whitewashed surfaces – whether white or coloured with pigment – faded unevenly. The low cost of materials involved allowed for frequent facelifts. And the same applies to modern colourwashes.

Tools

All you need to wash a wall is a bucket – in which to mix the paint – a good-sized paintbrush (at least 100 mm/4 in) and a roll of stockinette to mop up dribbles and soften brush strokes if desired. A coarse-haired limewash brush may also be used to stipple over brush strokes. For pure water washes which do not contain paint, it is easier to use a sponge or rag rather than a brush.

Some professional decorative painters work with two brushes – one wet to apply the wash and one dry to soften and work in any drips. Unless you are confidently ambi-

Above: Walls washed with yellow ochre pigment and water.
Below: A corner of my own living room washed with a peachy-tan colour and water 8:1.

dextrous, stick to a cloth and one paintbrush.

Before you start work, cover the floor with some form of protection. Newspapers are useful, although if a room is carpeted, a waterproof dust sheet of some kind is a better idea. Most DIY stores sell thin polythene dustsheets in handy packs. Make sure all walls are accessible, as once you start, it will not take long to complete the first coat.

Effect

To achieve the attractive dappled finish so characteristic of colourwashing, it is necessary to apply at least two uneven layers of diluted paint, so creating a soft impression of colour. Each consecutive wash thereafter will deepen the final tone of your surface.

The degree you have diluted your paint mixture as well as the way it is applied will both affect the finish. A wash can look like softly mottled parchment or it can look obviously brushy. Generally, the thicker the wash, the more brushy it will appear; and the less you soften your brush strokes, the more obvious it will be. The choice is yours.

An oil-based glaze may be used successfully to achieve the free, brushy version of washing which interiors writer Jocasta Innes calls 'under-the-brush'. A similar effect can be achieved with emulsion paint which is much faster-drying. This can create a really 'textured' effect to give the impression of a roughly-hewn cottage wall.

Technique

Once the wash is thoroughly blended, apply it to your surface with crossways brush movements, leaving obvious areas (about 40 per cent) of your ground untouched. It is important to get rid of any dribbles as you work. Keep checking on the previously painted area as runs are not always immediately noticeable. Wiping dribbles usually adds to the effect of shading, although it is important not to cover the base coat completely.

Try to apply the wash with rhythmic brush strokes (music may help you keep your rhythm) and do not worry if the first coat looks insipid and wishy-washy. Initial unevenness is important for a good final effect.

Once the first coat is completely dry (and it does not take long, especially if it is well diluted and the weather is warm), the next coat can be applied. Repeat the whole procedure, this time covering your base coat (ground) and portions of the first coat. Still watch for dribbles, taking care not to soften the whole effect as you remove them.

Stand back and look at your handiwork from time to time. If you spot drips when the wash is already touch dry, wet your brush with water and manipulate gently. This has the effect of diluting the area and dispersing the dribbles of paint.

An acrylic varnish should only be applied when the wash is completely dry. To be safe, wait for about 48 hours.

A lovely cloudy pink effect was achieved by washing these walls with emulsion diluted with water. The wash also camouflages ugly plaster patterns on the walls.

COLOURWASHING

1. Unevenly brush on the watery wash.

2. Leave obvious areas unpainted.

3. When dry, paint a second coat.

4. You have a lovely mottled surface.

RUBBING

The effect of rubbed colour may be similar to colourwashing when applied to walls. Although it lacks the brushiness, it has a lovely polished lustre.

Rubbing a glaze over a smooth surface creates a soft, uneven cloud of colour. For amateurs, it is wonderfully easy to do and for professionals, it provides a technique which, coupled with others, can help create sophisticated and magical effects.

At its simplest, rubbing is an extension of household polishing. Oil-based glazes are gently rubbed onto a smooth base coat or ground (preferably oil-based eggshell). The inevitable unevenness which results creates a quiet, tonal contrast. This helps to suggest the faded feel of age. One or more

Luxurious furnishings, antique furniture and collections of art look quite natural and elegant against a sensitively rubbed wall surface.

layers of glaze can be applied, and the colour will intensify with each coat. For this reason it is best to start with a light tone and then build it up slowly, until the required effect is achieved. It may take a little longer, but there will be added depth to the surface, contributing to the charm and atmosphere of the room.

Technique

You can use a commercial glaze (which should be diluted with turpentine and mixed with a little oil-based eggshell), or a good home-made glaze. We have found that the appropriately coloured eggshell, boiled linseed oil and pure turpentine oil mixed 2:2:3 works wonders.

1. Paint on a dilute glaze mixture.

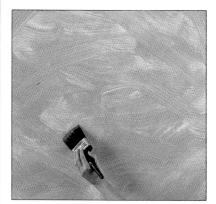

2. Cover the entire surface area.

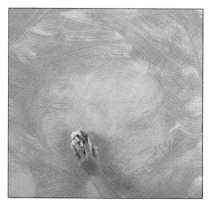

3. Rub gently as if you are polishing.

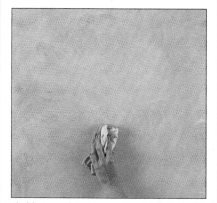

4. Use a circular motion to finish off.

Numerous coats of tinted glaze were rubbed into these flaking walls.

Brushed on and wiped off with rags dampened with white spirit, the effect is soft and mottled like colourwashing. Use a circular motion to soften edges as you would when polishing.

The main difference between this technique and colourwashing with an oil-based glaze is the addition of linseed oil for rubbing. The oil makes the glaze malleable, allowing you to gradually rub away more colour where desired. However, it slows down the drying process by at least 24 hours.

Variations

By extending this basic technique of colour rubbing, it is possible to achieve interesting effects on wood.

Relief rubbing Carved furniture and mouldings benefit greatly from an adaption of colour rubbing. To achieve a naturally weathered look adding shadow and relief, universal undercoat, diluted eggshell or thick glaze is painted onto the surface and then rubbed off, usually when slightly tacky. Colour should remain in all the crevices adding depth, character and a timeless look of age.

Grain rubbing Undistinguished wood can be treated in the same way, provided it has an open grain. Soft, light-hued woods, like pine, are best.

Fake liming Universal undercoat or a liming gilp (see page 91) painted on and then rubbed off furniture or floorboards has a similar effect to traditional liming giving a worn, weathered look.

Again soft, light woods are a prerequisite. A more pronounced effect is achieved if the grain is 'lifted' prior to applying paint. To do this, bleach with a commercial wood bleach or lightener and rub with a wire brush. Finish with water and sand lightly.

SPATTERING

Spattering may be used to create a number of different effects on its own or in conjunction with other techniques. It is a quick and easy way to jazz up a flat, dull surface.

Spattered paint can be used to create texture, to add colour, or to produce a range of effects useful for imitating granite, stonework, porphyry, the gold speckles in lapis lazuli finishes, and even to create a spottiness in some types of marble.

Basically all one aims to do is to shower flecks of paint onto the surface. Although the effect is a random one, it is essential to control the movement or you will end up with splashes and splodges which look plain messy. Both the distance you are from the surface and the tool you choose to

A combination of techniques on a variety of surfaces, including black spattering on the table, chairs and on the ragged and varnished walls.

use will affect your splattered finish. Colour, too, will have a marked influence. A mass of large bold-coloured spots will look lively and bright whereas subtle shades spattered in a contained manner (as in granite) will look more subdued and sophisticated.

Technique

Any stiff-bristled brush may be used, although for detailed work, a stencil brush or even a toothbrush is particularly suitable. An ordinary paintbrush should be dipped into paint and then knocked against a stick of some sort to create the spatter. A stencil brush may be treated in the same way, but for a toothbrush, run your thumb across the bristles.

Left top: Spattering creates interest and depth on an ordinary frame.
Left bottom: A pair of bottles and an unusual home-made table have all been spattered for an interesting and unusual effect.
Above: Stylishly spattered, this classically designed side table is a feature.

SPATTERING

1. Hit your brush against a stick.

2. Little speckles cover the surface.

Flicking the brush in a more jerky manner will cause streaked lines of paint rather than spots. This is fine if you want to create a wild, rather less subtle effect.

Paint

Emulsions, acrylics or gloss paints may be used for spattering. If you are working with an oil-based medium, you should dilute the paint with turpentine, but make absolutely certain the surface is bone dry as the effect of turpentine on a wet, painted or glazed surface will cause cissing (see box on this page).

Although it is quite possible to spatter vertical surfaces like walls, it is advisable to practise on a flat, horizontal surface first.

Precautions

Spattering can be a messy business, so take precautions against splashing onto other surfaces. Put plenty of newspaper on the floor and mask adjacent surfaces. Portable pieces should be removed to an area where paint splashes will not matter.

Effect

The closer you are to your surface the smaller the spots will be. For spots of a similar size, hit your stick in the same place, with the same impetus, each time. If is a good idea to test your spatter pattern and size on a piece of paper before you start.

Used over other techniques, especially soft stippling or sponging, spattering can create a sophisticated look.

CISSING

Closely related to spattering is cissing, which is particularly effective when used with beige and raw umber to create an earthy fossilstone finish. Straight solvent or a mixture of paint and solvent is flicked or spattered onto the wet surface, effectively opening the paint into tiny translucent pools. These can be softened with a hake brush or badger softener. You will find that different solvents have different effects, so experiment with turpentine, white spirit, methylated spirits and even water.

MARBLING

Imitation marbling is one of the most exciting paint techniques there is. The effects achieved range from faithful accuracy to dramatic fake.

Traditional marbling was done by an élitist group of craftsmen who were able to reproduce the real thing with stunning accuracy. However, modern marbling is well within the scope of amateur decorators.

Certainly it is one of the more ambitious finishes, but once mastered, can be quite addictive. Furthermore, when you aim simply for a fantasy effect, marbling is fun, and quite impressive effects can be achieved with ease in a surprisingly short space of time.

The origins of marbling go back to an-

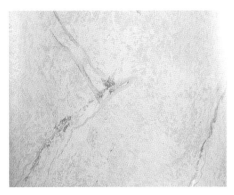

A particularly dramatic finish for an internal door which is marbled in gold and black to mirror sections of a real marble entrance-hall floor.

cient time with stylised examples found on Mycenaean pottery from 2200 BC and there is evidence that it was used in ancient Egypt. It reached a peak of popularity in the nineteenth century, with enthusiastic Victorians covering every conceivable surface with marbling, woodgraining and patterned wallpaper.

Magical marbling effects may be created in a multitude of ways for walls, floors, precast concrete furniture, ceilings – in fact for just about any surface there is.

There are countless varieties of real marble, all of which may provide inspiration. All our major centres boast public buildings with lavish, marble-tiled entrance halls and floors. Keep your eyes open for the

colours and styles you admire most and then examine the different tones within one type, trace the irregular veins and natural striations of the stone, and absorb the surreal quality real marble so often imparts. You will realise that fact can be stranger than fake.

Then consider simulated marbled varieties. Here the options are limitless. By employing a combination of techniques you have probably already mastered, you can achieve stunning effects. Above all, do not be intimidated: even some of the most naïve marbling attempts look quite impressive.

Technique

Much contemporary painted marbling is stylised, rather than a simulated copy of the real material. Even colours may be totally unrealistic. Whichever look you want, there are a multitude of methods to take you there. Irrespective of the tricks you employ, you must follow a basic procedure. First paint a suitable coloured ground; then apply and distress a glaze; and finally embellish your work with veins and other streaks and flecks.

Paint

While marbled finished are created with both oil-based and emulsion paints, I firmly believe that the best results are achieved with oils. Water-based paints dry so fast that it is impossible to blend the veins and other markings, so the final effect becomes an impressionistic painting rather than a breathtaking imitation.

Italian art graduate, Tiziana Giardini, who normally prefers emulsions to create stylised wispy veins with ostrich feathers, has also achieved remarkable floating marble effects with a combination of the two paint types, literally floating oils on water. If you like the idea, experimentation is your best bet. Defy the proven methods and you may be surprised by the result.

Ground Generally the basecoat or ground for marbling is a lighter tone than the glaze which covers it; white for grey, pale green for deep verdite marble, and pale, creamy yellow for an ochre variation. However, this is not a hard-and-fast rule, as stylised black marbling proves. Here a black eggshell base is dabbed with greys and white for effect, resulting in a quite fantastic final impression.

Glazes The modern tradition often employs a mixture of commercial scumble glaze, turpentine and oil-based eggshell paint (1:1:1). However, our standard 2:2:1

scumble glaze (page 91) works wonders every time. I like this adaption of eggshell, which I tint myself, purified linseed oil (prepared for artists) and turpentine oil. The latter is available from specialist stores including a few hardware dealers, or from pharmacies. It smells pleasant and is somehow smoother to work with. It is also used by some artists.

It is a good idea to mix two or three tones of glaze, to enable you to get a realistically variable finish. Once painted on and distressed, then softened so the shades merge softly into one another, you can add veins and striations. To a large extent, it pays to mimic the appearance of real marble, after all even the stylised versions are a kind of imitation.

Veins These may be painted in with a thin, pointed artists' brush using universal tinters or artists' oils. If you choose oils, squeeze a small amount into a saucer and add just a drop or two of turpentine to thin them out to the correct consistency.

Veins may also be produced with feathers (the traditional tool was a goose feather), putting the paint on or removing it with turpentine.

Top: Wonderfully realistic marble pillars and balusters created by sponging and painting in acrylics.
Above: Marbled with glazes.
Below: Six different kinds of real marble prove that fact can sometimes be far stranger than fake.

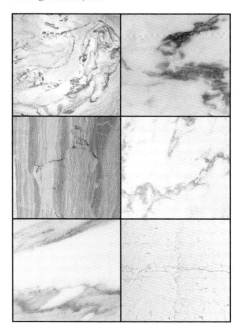

MARBLING

1. Roughly paint on the glaze.

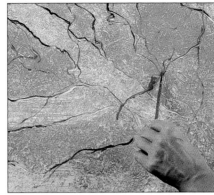
5. Cross these with lighter veins.

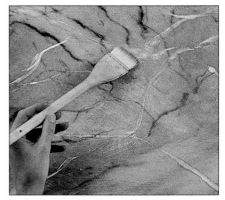
9. Soften the feathered-in veins.

2. Dab with bunched-up newspaper.

6. Gently soften with mutton cloth.

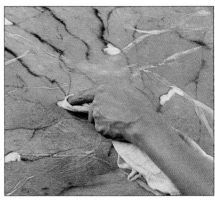
10. Remove tiny islands of colour.

3. Drag a brush through for effect.

7. Now soften the veins with a brush.

11. Ciss with white spirit.

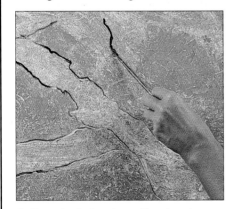
4. Draw in dark veins with a brush.

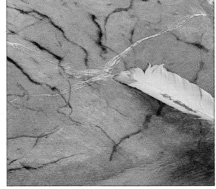
8. Dip a feather in turpentine.

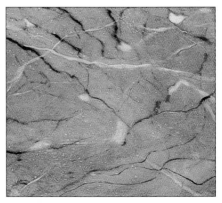
12. Soften for a realistic finish.

An ordinary kitchen with wooden cupboards is transformed with marbling.

Distressing

In this context, 'distressing' refers very specifically to the technique of breaking up the ground for marbling (rather than simulating wear and tear). A variety of methods may be employed while the glaze is still wet.

Rags A rag will soften your brush strokes.

Brushes A coarse-haired block brush or specialist stippling brush may be used to stipple the surface.

Sponges A marine sponge works in the same way as rags, and may be used to sponge on the glaze rather than applying with a paintbrush.

Newspapers Old newspaper can be a wonderful tool, especially if you are working with a pale marble. Choose a page with lots of black print and you will find that its seeping black ink adds a surprising effect. The glaze must be very wet or the ink will not be affected.

White spirit Small drops of white spirit will cause cissing (creating small craters) which may be an effective distressing technique for some marbles.

Cling film or plastic wrap Placed over the wet glaze and quickly removed, cling film or plastic wrap leaves an interesting almost ragged impression.

Blotting paper A long piece of blotting paper crushed in your hand can help achieve gloriously effective cracks – quite different to those achieved with feathers.

Finishing off

A few finishing touches complete the effect.

Veining Drawing in the veins takes a certain skill as it is easy to overdo the effect at this stage. Colours, too, should be reasonably believable with earthy hues coming into their own again: especially the umbers and siennas.

Following the natural diagonal lines, draw varying lines across the surface to simulate cracks, gently softening with a hake brush as you go. Take care not to smudge the veins out of existence and keep your movements light or you will start to get streaky brush marks. (If you can lay your hands on a badger softener this task will be simplified, as these super-soft brushes polish as they soften.)

Continue fidgeting in smaller veins until you are happy with the effect. For realistic effects, avoid heavy parallel lines and cobweb patterns.

Islands Once the veining is complete, it is possible to remove tiny 'islands' of colour with a cloth-covered finger.

Sealing Real marble has a marvellous sheen which may be achieved by sealing your work when it is completely dry (preferably after 48 hours). A clear polyurethane varnish, diluted with white spirit, is a possibility for certain colours. However, it does yellow, sometimes drastically altering the effect. Alternatively use a 'milk varnish' (a mixture of varnish, turpentine and a little white eggshell) to seal and, at the same time, tone down the marble. Or coat with clear acrylic sealer which will protect without yellowing and at the same time provide the sheen you need.

Surfaces

Before you choose your surface, consider where real marble is generally used. It is a heavy material, and on floors and walls would be divided into panels, slabs or tiles. Frames, mouldings, precast concrete pillars and balusters, fireplace surrounds and even table tops all make suitable subjects.

Panelling

To achieve a panelled or a tiled effect, it is necessary to divide your surface into sections before marbling begins. For this, measuring is essential and a scaled drawing always helps. The panels may be drawn in with a soft pencil or masked.

To paint, work on alternate sections and wait until these have dried before filling in the remaining sections. A more impressionistic panelled effect may be created by gluing braid to the wall surface once the marbling is dry.

STENCILLING

Stencilling is a wonderful craft which has its origins in ancient civilisations. Simple to master and satisfying to execute, it is amazingly effective as a decorating tool.

Stencilling is cheap, easy and effective. By mastering a few simple techniques, you can transform a dull room into something special in just a few hours.

Although the origins of this technique are reflected in country crafts, stencilling can be sophisticated and exciting, adding originality, colour and pattern, rather than a stylised cottage look. At the same time, this is the simplest way to achieve a fresh country feel. The secret is in the design you choose, in its application, and in the medium used to apply it.

A blue painted floor with intricate basket designs and a grid pattern borrowed from the wallpaper borders used on the bedroom walls.

Pre-cut stencils, brushes, stencil crayons and paints are available at most DIY stores as well as specialist decorating shops. Several books featuring stencil patterns and ready-to-use stencils are also obtainable; and of course it is possible to design and cut your own (see page 93 for suppliers and page 95 for further reading list).

Design

The source of inspiration for stencil designs is limitless. Fabrics, wallpapers, quilts, ceramics, architectural mouldings, natural forms, like leaves and fruit, even birds and animals, may suggest a motif.

Before you start, decide on a design and draw it on plain white card or paper. If you

feel you cannot draw your own patterns, copy one you like and, if necessary, enlarge it with a photostat machine. Alter it if you wish, but it is essential to keep your outlines simple.

In stencilling, everything must be reduced to a series of basic outlines which are filled in with colour. A simple shape becomes a cutout of each separate section; so an intricate botanical specimen becomes a series of interesting configurations. To do this you will have to leave adequate 'bridges' between each shape; but once you start, you will find it is quite easy to think in stencilled outlines, converting everything into simple forms.

Your final design will depend largely on the surface you plan to stencil and the effect you wish to achieve. Floors, furniture and walls all demand a different approach. Also, when designing friezes and borders, you will have to take the repeat pattern into account. Tracing paper is a useful aid for doing this. Simply trace the design several times to make sure it works. If it does not, make any alterations before cutting the stencil.

Materials

Stencilling is, in essence, so simple that the materials required are minimal. While some specialised pieces of equipment, including brushes and quick-drying stencil paints, do make the task at hand easier, it is quite acceptable to improvise or find substitutes.

A variety of reuseable materials may be used for stencilling, although the most acceptable and readily available are oiled stencil card and transparent plastic film. All can be cut with a craft, hobby or utility trimming knife. To ensure a good, clean outline, it helps to cut on a self-healing cutting board. However, it does not matter if your cut edges are not perfect, as the stencilled outlines will be slightly softened when brushed.

Oiled card Brown stencil card is quite durable and easy to cut. You can trace your design directly onto it, but because you cannot see through the card, it is sometimes difficult to position for repeat patterns.

Transparent film Acetate and PVC film are manufactured in several gauges. The thicker the sheeting, the more difficult it is to cut. Both products are more expensive than card, but have the advantage of transparency, making it simple to position for repeats. If you buy a roll of film, cut it into sheets and lie them flat (under a heavy book) before using. Although you cannot

draw on transparent film with regular pencils or felt-tipped pens, you can use markers manufactured for writing on shiny surfaces.

Semi-transparent film Mylar, developed by Americans Adele Bishop and Cile Lord in the 1970s, is frequently used for pre-cut stencils. Unlike acetate, it can be printed and written on. You can also buy Mylar with pre-printed grid lines, especially for stencilling. Similar film is used for pre-cut kit stencils.

Washable melamine Also semi-transparent and flexible, washable melamine is used for some British stencils, including several produced by Jocasta Innes.

Opaque film Although not readily available through retail outlets, white sheets of non-expanded polystyrene work well for stencilling. Like oiled card, it is not easy to position for repeats.

A combination of three colours – pale blue, turquoise-green and dark peach – has been used for these walls with stencilled designs.

Paints

Special quick-drying stencil paints and stencil crayons are available in most DIY stores as well as specialist decorating shops. There are also many quite acceptable alternatives. The effect you achieve will depend largely on the paint you choose to use, but its consistency as well as the quantity you load on your brush will also affect the final impression.

Stencil paints These are quick-drying, water based paints, specially designed for stencilling. Available in a wide range of colours they are quite economical as they can be used sparingly to create a soft, cloudy effect. Stencil paints can also be mixed together easily to make any shade you wish.

Stencil crayons Large, oil-based crayons that produce a soft effect when applied with a brush. They are easy for the novice as there is no danger of runny paint leaking under the stencil. The colours also blend beautifully.

Acrylic paints Water-based artists' acrylics, available in a wide range of colours, are ideal for stencilling on most surfaces. Subtle shading may be difficult as acrylics produce solid colour and form a tough skin when dry. It is essential to wipe your stencil clean as you work to avoid a build-up of paint. Rinse brushes as soon as painting is complete.

Right above: Stencilled wisteria from the Jocasta Innes Painted Garden series. Below: Subtle stencilling gives a very ordinary door its own unique style.

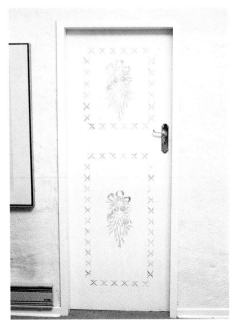

Poster paints An advantage of poster paint, which dries to a waterproof finish, is its relatively low cost and wide availability. Because it is water-based, it can be diluted to achieve a beautifully shaded effect. These will need to be sealed when dry.

Artists' watercolours Although watercolours would seem to be an impractical medium for stencilling, the translucent, shaded effects you can create are lovely. Mix colours and dilute with water, but use sparingly. When absolutely dry, seal with an acrylic varnish for permanence.

Emulsion Ordinary matt or silk emulsion paint may be used for stencilling. It may be used as it is or thinned to make shading easier. To get a bold and solid effect of colour, add a little interior filler to thicken your paint.

Gloss paints If you are working on a surface which has been painted with an oil-based paint, ordinary gloss paints may be used undiluted for stencilling. An eggshell based glaze (see page 91) may be sponged on for a more subtle effect.

Artists' oils Small quantities of artists' oils are useful for colouring oil glazes. Special quick-drying artists' oils are available for stencilling on fabric, wood, paper and porcelain.

Aerosol cans Those who successfully use spray paints seldom revert to using stencil brushes. They are quick-drying and versatile and you can use them on virtually any surface – even on appliances like fridges. Don't limit yourself to ordinary spray paint – car spray paint works equally well.

Fabric paints A selection of paints is available for stencilling on fabric. Usually these must be heat-sealed when dry to make the decorated fabric washable. A water-based range from Germany (Javana) manufactured for painting on silk may be used on other surfaces, and is particularly effective to colour wood, without concealing the grain.

Tools

The method you choose to apply your paint will have a major effect on the final image. Use whichever works best for you.

Stencil brushes Various sizes of stubby, stiff-bristled stencil brushes are available from specialist art shops and most DIY stores. Softer, hog-bristle brushes and even good shaving brushes can be used.

A dreary little bathroom was given a magical makeover for a television series on paint effects.

Sponges Marine sponges are a good alternative to stencil brushes and they enable you to work with great speed. Synthetic sponges and even rags can be substituted for the real thing; or improvise by tying foam in a ball-shape around a pencil for a handy applicator. Alternatively, craft and hobby shops sometimes have foam-topped sticks (for applying varnish) which are quite useful.

Low-tack masking tape is useful for sticking your stencil in position. It can then be lifted off and re-positioned without causing any damage to the existing surface.

When using aerosols, it is advisable to position your stencils with spray adhesive.

Technique

Stencilling is an art form, and as such does not demand absolute accuracy. If necessary, small smudges and mistakes are easily rectified by overpainting and anyway they often do not show in the overall scheme. More important is the method of application and colour chosen for the work.

Lovely effects can be created with pattern, by repeating the stencil to form an architectural frieze or even a simplified trompe l'oeil. This repetition will also help unify the room.

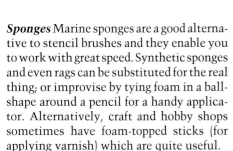

Various effects achieved with different paints including emulsion (above left and centre right), stencil crayons (top left), quick-drying artists' oils (top right), silk paints (centre left) and watercolours (above right).

Above: An old laundry converted into a delightful haven for a child, with custom-cut stencils echoing the parrot pattern on the colourful blinds.

Left: A beautifully stencilled floor, which has seen many years of use, is stencilled and painted with emulsion paints and sealed with acrylic varnish.

Colour

As with all decorative paint effects, the correct combination of background and stencil colour is vital to the finished effect you want to create. Generally it is easier to succeed with dark colour stencilled over a pale background, although (in total contradiction) some of the nicest stencilling I have seen has been pastel and white over a deep ground.

The background surface may be white, a solid colour, softly washed or heavily textured broken colour; each has its advantages and will contribute to the final picture. Whatever the choice, the impact of your background must be taken into account when the stencil colour is selected.

It is wise to choose colours with basic furnishings in mind, although they may contrast, complement or even provide an accent.

Shading and contrast

While some people do prefer solid blocks of stencilled colour, it is simple to achieve delicate contrasts and shading when stencilling. I have identified three basic techniques, each of which is dependent on the method of application.

Stencil brushes When you are brushing on a stencilled design, it is the paint which will be largely responsible for the degree of shading you can achieve. Stencil paints are designed to allow you to achieve a crisply outlined print which is delicately shaded. This is an effect older children often aspire to when colouring in with wax crayons.

By stencilling the design three or four times without reloading the brush with paint, you will achieve a series of three or four prints, each successively lighter than the last. This adds to the contrast and hand-painted effect of the whole.

Sponges Soft sponging or stippling can create a good effect although shading may be difficult. Sponging may also be used as a second step: to soften solid blocks of colour previously stencilled. Simply choose a lighter tone of colour and lightly sponge over your original print.

Whether sponging or brushing, your tool should be quite dry. You can always go over the pattern to darken if necessary.

Aerosol cans Spray painting is an excellent medium for achieving tonal contrast. This happens two ways: by mixing colour and by varying pressure when spraying. In addition, a series of lightly sprayed coats will build up colour gradually, achieving further contrast.

Pattern

The actual design as well as its application will contribute to the final pattern each stencil produces.

Walls If a motif is to be used as an architectural border or frieze, a repeat pattern becomes important. Ideally, any repeat should be considered before painting begins. This will avoid a jarring break in the overall design when you suddenly get to the corner of a room.

Measure from the centre of your wall and determine how many repeats are required. Often you will be able to juggle the arrangement of stencils to accommodate the repeats, simply by increasing the gaps between each shape. If not, you may have to incorporate an additional design in the centre of your wall.

Floors Proper handling of a repeat pattern is absolutely vital when an allover pattern is to be produced on a continuous surface like a floor. The only way you can do this is to mark a grid on your floor allowing for the borders required. Approach the project as you would a patchwork quilt and you are sure to succeed.

STENCILLING

1. To cut, place the acetate on glass.

4. Line up for a repeat pattern design.

2. Cut a new stencil for each colour.

5. When dry, apply the next colour.

3. Apply paint with a dry brush.

6. Reposition for the third colour.

RELATED ALTERNATIVES

Apart from traditional stencilling, various forms of printing may also be used for decorating. Simple potato prints can be used to create charming patterns for wall friezes, door panels or even for decorating furniture. A variety of other fruit and vegetables may also be used, although root vegetables are generally best. Wood blocks, foam shapes and rubber stamps may be employed for the same technique. Particularly good for printing geometric designs, they may be used with ink or paint. Spraying colour through lace or paper doillies can also be effective as this creates pretty lacey designs, too detailed to stencil in the conventional way. For a reverse form of stencilling, especially appropriate for furniture, use ferns, ivy leaves, in fact anything with an attractive, clear defined form as a template. Stipple over the top of the plants and you will be left with their delicate and lovely natural shapes.

MURALS

Murals are a most beautiful way of decorating interiors. Ideas and inspiration can come from a million different sources and the results may be as simple or sophisticated, small or large as you wish.

Wall paintings of various kinds have been popular for hundreds of years. While some undoubtedly remain the domain of professionals, basic yet distinctive, paintings may be created with surprisingly little skill.

For centuries friezes, frescoes and panels have been painted in a multitude of locations; and entire walls and ceilings have been embellished with incredibly beautiful works of art.

Wall paintings have been found in Egyp-

A delightfully stylised mural behind a cosy private bar introduces a Japanese theme – with a group of languid oriental maidens, a garden and a lily pond.

tian tombs; in the ancient remains of Pompeii; in Italian chapels and villas built in the fifteenth and sixteenth centuries and in historic seventeenth-century English manor houses. Even good hardwood panelling was decorated with pictures in the sixteenth century.

Not surprisingly, a number of modern wall paintings incorporated into interior design are found in children's rooms: bold expressions of colour which seldom fail to delight.

Children love fantasy and so the subject matter is endless. Balloons, rainbows, nursery-rhyme and fairy-tale characters, traffic signs, and animals all make ideal themes.

However more sophisticated murals call

for a more adult approach. Your child may enjoy living with Winnie the Pooh on the wall, but will you?

Start by looking at pictures of classical and traditional murals for inspiration. Look at paintings and tapestries, tiles and screens, remembering that any mural you paint will become a part of its surroundings. It may also dominate the room in which it is painted. Choose a subject you are comfortable with – and one which you can realistically tackle.

Technique

While some artists paint directly onto their wall surface with little prior planning, this is not advisable.

Most books give terrifying grids for wall paintings. Basic pictures and designs are divided into small squares and then translated into larger squares drawn to scale on the wall. While this is a foolproof method and advisable for amateur 'trompe l'oeil', beginners can start with simpler designs utilising home-made templates. These can be cut from medium-grade cardboard and then used to create pictures and patterns.

Look for strong, bold images, which can be easily translated into simple shapes. Once separated like this thay can be made into templates then placed on the wall to recreate a simplified picture of the original.

My first mural was based on the theme of my son's Moby Dick curtaining, chosen with a wall painting in mind. The outlines – a whale, shark's fin, flowers, shells, palm trees – were all simple and easy to copy. Every colour was translated into a different template so that each shape would be separate on the wall. The templates were not absolutely accurate, but once applied to the wall's surface (in a totally unplanned composition), looked incredibly effective. What did help, was accurate colour matching of the emulsion paints used.

If your picture design cannot be translated into simple templates and you cannot draw the picture freehand on the wall, see if it is possible to borrow a slide or overhead projector and copy the outlines in pencil on the wall.

Paint

Straightforward murals usually rely on flat, bold colour for impact. If you are using templates it is easy: simply paint in the shapes with acrylics, poster paints, emulsion or gloss paints as you would in a colouring book. It does not matter if the flatness of the wall is emphasised in a mural.

However, the use of glazes and washes, as well as simple sponging and stippling, can help increase depth and interest, especially

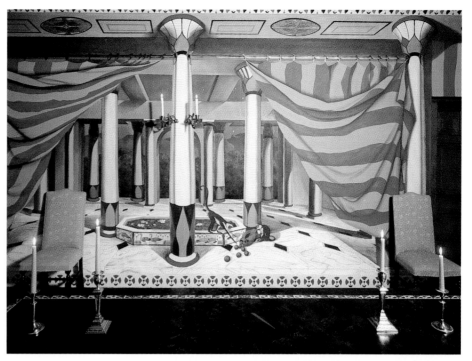

in background colour. For instance, a cloudy, blue sky effect can be created by sponging or by spraying pale blue paint onto a white background from an aerosol can; while the effect of trees can be created by stippling within a broad outline or by painting solid colour within a mass of leafy shapes.

Top: A maze of Egyptian columns, a lily pond and a couple of playful monkeys add a theatrical air of mystery to a room. Above: Bricks painted white and then rubbed with a coloured glaze provide an unobtrusive, mellow backdrop for a naïvely painted feline mural.

TROMPES L'OEIL

Trompe l'oeil is a French phrase which means to fool or deceive the eye. To succeed, the results should be realistic and this takes talent and skill. This is the reason why many of the best trompe l'oeil paintings have been created by professional painters, fine arts graduates and graphic designers.

You will find that palm trees painted (or even stencilled) on either side of a front door add colour and character to the entrance; a pastel-toned dhurrie rug painted in the centre of a living room gives warmth and a feeling of comfort; and tropical plants painted in a conservatory add freshness even when the plants are at their worst.

A trompe l'oeil pathway creates a new dimension in a passage; while inside trompes l'oeil magically add visual space, bringing the river into view for diners.

Painted stonework, cracks and architectural features all set the tone of a room, while painted picture frames, bows and medallions create a certain style.

A sophisticated trompe l'oeil will make you feel as if you are catching a glimpse of a garden beyond a window, or a field of flowers. It will add a new (almost physical) dimension to your room although it is important that subject matter is credible.

At the same time, amateur artists with a talent for reasonably accurate still life can achieve amazing success. Copy fruit or a vase of flowers or paint a copper pot onto the door of your kitchen cupboard. You will find that the naïveté of an unstudied painting is often an enhancement rather

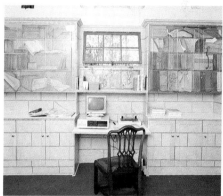

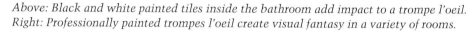

Above: Black and white painted tiles inside the bathroom add impact to a trompe l'oeil.
Right: Professionally painted trompes l'oeil create visual fantasy in a variety of rooms.

than a drawback. Or it may simply succeed as a visual joke.

The imitation of architectural features – skirting, cornices, dado rails and pillars – also qualifies as trompe l'oeil, and for simplicity, these can be masked or stencilled.

While paints used for any mural may be used to create a trompe l'oeil, professionals working in oil-based paints often use glazes in their work, distressing surfaces and incorporating the fantasy finishes described elsewhere in this book.

Technique

The success of a trompe l'oeil relies partly on the artist's ability to achieve a three-dimensional effect. Careful attention must therefore be given to colour, perspective, shading and contrast. Shadows are also important and the natural light source must always be taken into account.

Photographs and pictures from magazines and books can be helpful for painting a scene. For a more simple still life – perhaps flowers or fruit – nothing beats the real

thing. It helps to sketch your picture before you begin, and then work out a grid.

First make an accurate scale plan of your wall (or the area to be painted) and divide it into squares. The larger this plan, the easier it will be to see details of your design. Mark the squares on your wall and then transfer the outline. Unless your wall is white, chalk is a good medium for transferring the design. Otherwise use a soft pencil.

Paint

Like any work of art, there are no definite rules relating to the painting of a trompe l'oeil. However, the preparation of your background is important as an uneven surface is likely to ruin the illusion.

All paints vary in texture, translucency, opacity and colour intensity, so choose your medium with specific reference to your subject matter. It is inadvisable to use pure artists' oils – unless you mix them with driers (see page 90) – as they can take many months to dry thoroughly.

It helps to have a knowledge of artistic painting techniques as tonal contrast, shape and form are all vital. As always, colour – both translucent and opaque – is an important aid.

Seal a successful trompe l'oeil for protection. Use a matt acrylic varnish rather than polyurethane which yellows.

TORTOISESHELLING

Tortoiseshelling is a wonderfully rich decorative finish which has its origins in the Far East. It is particularly suitable for small surfaces including frames, boxes and lampstands.

Tortoiseshelling is not the easiest technique to master, but its distinctive effect is worth the trouble. Used over large surfaces, it can look sophisticated and dramatically striking: one of the strongest fantasy finishes around. But it must be done well.

First attempts should be limited to small, flat, surface areas like boxes, picture frames or, at most, small table tops. Large areas should be divided into panels to be really effective.

The decorative use of tortoiseshell dates back to Roman times when marine turtle shells were first imported into Europe from the Far East. Through the centuries they became increasingly expensive and difficult to obtain and so craftsmen began to fake the finish with paint.

Nowadays, real tortoiseshell is rarely found, but plastic hair combs and other small items are manufactured to look like tortoiseshell.

The colouring of realistic tortoiseshell ranges from golden brown and amber to deep red with almost black markings. It is also semi-translucent.

Technique

The most usual base coat colours for tortoiseshelling range from custard yellow, to yellow-orange and ochre, although

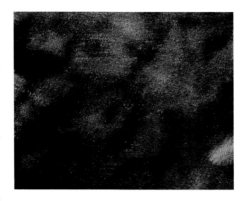

Painted tortoiseshell varies as much as the real thing. It looks best on lampstands, boxes, frames and bins.

a deep red may also be used. You can buy a ready-mixed colour or tint your own eggshell.

To create a tortoiseshell effect, one basically squeezes pure artists' oil onto varnish, linseed oil or a varnish-based glaze (sometimes called gilp) which has been painted onto the chosen ground. The oil paint must then be softened, lightly in various directions to achieve a mottled or stripy look. For realism, you must ensure that the stripes and blobs of colour go in a single diagonal direction or create a fan shape.

Various varnish mixtures can be used, but I have found a blend of clear varnish, turpentine and purified or boiled linseed oil (combined in the ratio 4:2:1) works well.

To get a golden colour, add a hefty squeeze of raw sienna artists' oil. Note, that unlike the distressed ground for marbling, a tortoiseshell surface should not be blotted or dabbed otherwise it will dry out much too quickly. Rather, the gilp helps the mixture spread.

For golden brown tortoiseshell, coat your yellow ground with the varnish or gilp and then paint a variety of markings over it with an artists' brush, using raw sienna, burnt sienna (which is reddish) and raw umber (which will give you a good dark colour). Vary the squiggles and blotches, creating overlapping islands with darker 'eye' spots, allowing them to fan outwards. Work fast as the paints do not take long to get tacky.

With a badger softener or hake watercolour brush, soften the whole surface by brushing on the diagonal, first in one direction (following the markings), then softly at different angles until all the edges are softened. Do not brush hard or you will get marks on your finished surface.

An alternative method is to rub a thin film of boiled linseed oil onto your ground and squeeze the oil paint directly onto this. This technique is recommended but be warned that it will take several days for the linseed oil to dry.

Once the surface is thoroughly dry, coat with a polyurethane varnish. This is one finish which usually benefits from any yellowing.

MALACHITE

The effect of painted malachite can be extraordinarily exotic. Although the finish looks elaborate, the technique it employs is disarmingly simple to master.

If you have ever examined a piece of malachite, you will know that it has strong patterns in an intense shade of green. As a paint effect, it is best reserved for small surfaces like boxes, picture frames and borders on tables. Once you have mastered the skill, a malachite finish can also look good on fashionable obelisks, corbels and lamp stands.

Although malachiting fits firmly within the confines of fantasy finishes, it helps to look at the real thing, if only for inspiration. Many curio shops sell malachite in some form or other. It is also incorporated into modern jewellery.

Technique

Your main tool for creating a malachite finish is going to be a piece of cardboard, roughly torn to enable you to create striations. Layered cardboard or art board – scored and then broken – works well. Alternatively work with whatever you have in the house as long as it is fairly thick and not too absorbent.

Your eggshell base coat must be a pale green: a lighter shade of the finished product. Artists' oils are used for the top coat, mixed with a small amount of gilp (see tortoiseshelling), a little artists' drying linseed oil or some scumble glaze.

Several greens can be used, although I like the effect of phthalo (spelled 'thalo' by some manufacturers) green mixed with a touch of lemon yellow. There are numerous alternatives and some variations you can try include viridian tinted with ultra-

Real malachite sells for vast sums of money, which is one reason for the popularity of painted pieces. It is best to paint small objects or boxes.

marine and just a hint of yellow ochre; or even a mix of lemon yellow and Prussian blue. Some professionals recommend Rowney's monestial green or a pure phthalo green.

The thick colour is then coated over your base and gently dabbed with stockinette to soften. Take a smallish piece of cardboard and begin by creating wavy lines which change direction, as well as the circles with are so characteristic of malachite. Change the cardboard as soon as the paint builds up on it. Smaller patterns can be made with a short-haired paintbrush.

When the oil paint is completely dry, coat with a non-yellowing acrylic varnish for protection.

Drag torn card through the oil paint.

LAPIS LAZULI

The imitation of this beautifully blue mineral is satisfyingly creative. As a fantasy finish, it is best used on small surfaces.

Nowadays lapis lazuli is seldom seen in large quantities and it is usually in the form of gemstones. This clear blue mineral which is speckled with tiny spots of 'fool's gold' was used in the fifteen century for its ultramarine-hued pigment. Nowadays, an amazingly effective imitation pigment is made from powdered fired clay, sodium carbonate, sulphur and resin.

Understandably, therefore, ultramarine artists' oils are the basis for a successful lapis lazuli paint effect. While purists use gold leaf for the speckled pyrites, gold powder or bright gold poster paint work reasonably well.

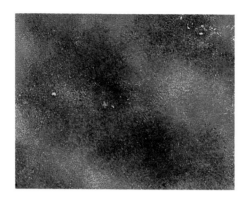

The deep blue lapis lazuli finish gives ordinary picture frames and boxes a luxurious look. It enriches cheap wooden candle holders and, combined with marbling, transforms a concrete orb.

Technique

Working on a medium blue (not too pale) ground, sponge on French ultramarine and bits of deep Prussian blue artists' oils to which a little gilp (see tortoiseshelling) or artists' drying linseed oil has been added. Alternatively mix scumble glaze with turpentine 2:1 and add about three times the amount of oil colour. To create depth, very softly sponge in cloudy patches of white. Then add a minute quantity of yellow ochre to create 'veins'. Soften with a brush.

Before the paint dries, blow on a little gold powder or dip an old toothbrush into gold paint, shake to remove the excess and then gently rub your thumb across the bristles to spatter. Alternatively (if you can afford it) rub gold leaf through a sieve and shake onto your surface.

Use an acrylic varnish once the surface is thoroughly dry. Note that polyurethane will yellow and therefore tend to throw a greenish cast.

BAMBOOING

The craze for bambooing furniture and accessories was one of many popular paint techniques in the 18th century and early Victorian era. Real bamboo was very expensive to buy and the passion for chinoiserie in the West necessitated an alternative.

Although it takes its inspiration from nature, it can also be translated into total fantasy.

The light-hearted technique of simulating bamboo is fun, if a little time-consuming, to employ. Bambooing works well on plain cane furniture, which is inexpensive and easy to come by.

Both simple bamboo and fabulously fake pieces can be painted with just a modicum of talent combined with time and effort. Find real bamboo and use it for inspiration.

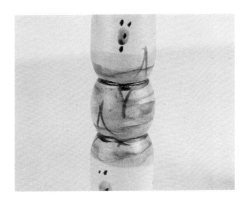

Both slavishly fake (below right) and stylised fantasy bamboo (above) can be used on frames and furniture. Colours may also be realistic or imaginary, as seen on this bamboo chair (below).

The most suitable subjects for bambooing are turned or cane furniture, rounded mouldings and light, wooden picture frames. A cast iron framework might also be suitable, as the beautifully painted staircase at Britain's Brighton Pavilion proves. Knots may be built up with putty, or simply painted on the surface.

Technique
The base coat for naturalistic, woody bamboo should be a straw colour although there is no reason why fake colours should not be used for the technique. Bambooed effects may also be painted directly onto light wood.

Any quick-drying paint medium may be used, but artists' acrylics over a silk emulsion base works well. Alternatively use an eggshell or satinwood ground detailed with tinted varnish (see page 91) and hobby enamels. Use fine artists' brushes for the detail.

A simple method is to paint a wide watery band of colour around the joints. Once dry, paint a second slightly narrower band of more intense colour within the first band. Then put thin lines of solid colour around the centre of each knot. Finally, add spines, eyes and freckles – all typical features of the real thing – for effect.

When the paint is completely dry, the 'bamboo' should be coated with matt or satin varnish for protection and to give a realistic sheen.

VINEGAR PAINTING

Vinegar painting, also called vinegar graining, is a brash, happy technique which was used by American furniture craftsmen in the nineteenth century.

Many cheap woods – old and new – make furniture a good vehicle for paint finishes, and vinegar graining is a particularly jolly effect to try.

Throughout the nineteenth century, country craftsmen applied a delightful fantasy finish to ordinary wooden pieces, often employing natural earthy colours. By rolling and dabbing linseed-oil putty over home-made vinegar glazes, bold and beautiful effects were created. Some were quite realistic, like bold woodgraining, others too vigorous to be true.

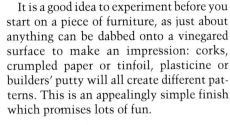

A variety of things may be used to create patterns in vinegar paint: including corks (above and below), plasticine (bottom left and right) and even crumpled paper.

It is a good idea to experiment before you start on a piece of furniture, as just about anything can be dabbed onto a vinegared surface to make an impression: corks, crumpled paper or tinfoil, plasticine or builders' putty will all create different patterns. This is an appealingly simple finish which promises lots of fun.

Technique

While traditional vinegar painting seems to have been done in good, honest, earthy colours over a pale ground, there is no reason to limit your effects. Try red over pink, midnight blue over powder blue, dark over light green – after all you might as well match your colour scheme.

Start by painting the surface with eggshell or satin wood in the paler tone. When dry, rub with fine, cloth-backed sandpaper.

Vinegar paint or glaze is made by first mixing powder pigments (see page 91) with a little brown malt vinegar to form a paste. Then add a mixture of about 150 ml (5 fl oz) vinegar, a teaspoon of sugar (to make it sticky) and a squeeze of washing-up liquid.

Wipe your surface with a rag moistened with vinegar and then paint on the glaze. When the surface is slightly tacky, start work. Play with your patterns and mix your tools if you wish.

The surface takes several hours to dry, and as it does, it loses some of its lustre. To restore the gleam, and protect the item of furniture, finish with several coats of polyurethane varnish.

WOODGRAINING

Woodgraining is an ancient, traditional art still practised by craftsmen all over the world. Generally cheap woods and other surfaces were, and still are, grained to simulate rate and expensive species.

It may seem bizarre to paint wood with a decorative wood finish, but it has been done for centuries; and with good reason.

The basis of this technique is to fake or imitate the grain and colour of certain prestigious woods – particularly mahogany, bird's-eye maple, oak and walnut – when you either cannot find or afford them.

Fake wood dates back centuries; evidence of Bronze Age pottery displays wood effects. More recent examples include woodgrained painted oak panelling exhibited in Britain's Victoria and Albert Museum which dates from 1600.

Woodgraining was exceptionally popular in France where *faux bois* was much in demand.

In the 1800s, the technique reached such a high standard that there were disputes whether a piece was fake of not!

The Victorians greatly favoured woodgraining and could even choose from a catalogue of different wood finishes.

Even in the 1930s, woodgraining was still in evidence, with pine being a popular wood to copy.

Technique

There is no reason why the basic woodgraining technique should not be translated into colourful fantasy finishes. Just for fun

Various styles include these intricate graining techniques (above and below) to the plywood-like ground for murals (bottom).

simply simulate the grain and change the colour.

You will find your starting point in dragging and combing, although the addition of knots and other markings is also essential. The major difference between dragging and woodgraining is the rather welcome addition of 'wobbling' in the latter. Look at a piece of wood and explore the natural grain and you will see how it changes its movement and flow.

To be really effective, it helps to have access to heartgrainers and rubber combs – but a more simplistic fantasy effect can be achieved with home-made substitutes made from cardboard or rubber squeegees. Corks, carved to form stamps, are also useful aids; and for the eyes in bird's-eye maple, there is nothing to beat knuckles (your own). If you want to simulate walnut, an adaption of malachiting (using a firm cloth instead of cardboard) works well to create clusters of knots.

A pencil brush (or any thin artists' brush) may be used to draw in the grain of certain woods, like oak.

The secret is to improvise until you get the effect you want.

Your base coat or ground colour will depend on the wood you want to simulate. For oaks, use a yellow ochre beige; red for bird's-eye maple; and burnt sienna for mahogany.

Paint on in the direction in which the grain will run and if the wood to be simulated is coarse, use coarse brush strokes.

Part Four
SUITABLE SURFACES

Most surfaces are suitable for decorative paint finishes; the challenge is to determine which technique will most enhance the surface you want to embellish.

There is little doubt that walls represent the largest surface area in any one room. This is also the most obvious place for experimentation. But floors, ceilings, woodwork and even your furniture may also prove to be paintable. In fact a dragged window frame, a stencilled floor or even a chair, simply sponged to match a cushion, might just prove to be the *pièce de résistance* in your decorating scheme.

Old surfaces may have to be disguised or adapted; certainly they will have to be suitably prepared. But there is little doubt that the effort will be worth it; in fact you will probably go back for more.

This magnificent hall is painted in the tradition of Pompeii. It features marbled pillars, sponged walls, stencilled dado rails, friezes, murals, a cloud panel on the ceiling, as well as a gloriously stencilled and hand-painted floor. Even the table in the centre of the entrance has been treated with paint.

PREPARING TO PAINT

While decorative painting is fun, the necessary preparation can be dull, time-consuming and even tedious. Whether you are planning to paint walls, floors, ceilings, doors or furniture, the drudgery of proper preparation cannot be ignored.

Although preparation is the most tiresome part of decorating, it simply cannot be avoided. Without it you are likely to end up with tatty results and hours of wasted effort. Even if you are faced with a sound new surface, you are going to have to spend time applying the correct undercoats to ensure you start with a properly prepared ground.

If the prospect of this tedium puts you off, just consider the heartbreak of seeing your decorative efforts crumble and peel. Persevere, it will be worth it.

WALLS

Although your walls do not have to be perfect, just about every decorative paint finish requires a clean, even base. At the very least this will mean a good dusting or a thorough scrub with sugar soap.

Flaky paint should be scraped and sanded; cracks and holes from picture hooks and nails must be filled; shabby plaster should be removed and replaced; and damp dealt with. If you have severe problems, consider calling in the experts.

Before you start the actual paint work, remove all plug and light switch plates, as well as any wall-mounted light fittings, and mask any areas you want to keep free of paint or glaze. Although a glaze is easily wiped clean if tackled when still wet, the alternative is to spend time laboriously touching up smudges and drips later.

Paint The most effective way to clean a grimy painted surface is to scrub with a sugar soap solution. Follow the manufacturer's instructions and work from top to bottom so that mucky water does not dribble onto your cleaned surface.

You are unlikely to have to strip paint off a wall unless you are faced with multiple layers of gloss paint which is blistering and flaking. Even if the surface was previously varnished or sealed with polyurethane, you can usually overpaint with universal undercoat rather than strip it.

If an area has been filled, as soon as the filler is dry, sand lightly and cover with a universal undercoat before painting proper begins. Cellulose fillers like Polyfilla are highly absorbent and will result in patches on your finished surface if they are not sealed.

Wallcovering Wallpaper should be stripped, although I have seen successful overpainting and subsequent ragging done on quite a shabby base. Remember though, while some decorative paint finishes can help camouflage irregular, uneven and even ugly surfaces, flaws and bumps may be accentuated.

If you are removing a vinyl wallcovering, it will probably be possible to peel away the top layer and then paint over the paper lining which remains. To remove an ordinary wallpaper, douse with warm water and then strip with a scraper. Really stubborn paper can be removed with a proprietary stripping solution or an electric steam stripper.

Plaster If your home is new or you have had to replaster wall areas, be sure to allow the new plaster to dry thoroughly before you do any decorative painting.

FLOORS

Of all surfaces, floors take the biggest beating. For this reason it is advisable to consider all your options before deciding to paint.

Several paint finishes can be used successfully and most effectively on floors, and your preparation will, to a large degree, depend on which one you choose. Marbling over a slightly chipped concrete base might, for instance, improve the final effect.

Concrete If you are planning a granite, fossilstone or marble finish, odd gouges and imperfections can add to its authenticity. But if you want to stencil or paint a trompe l'oeil carpet, you would be advised to repair the surface.

The experts warn of potential problems in long-term bonding between the screed and paint. This is because fine, powdery cement tends to come to the surface, making adhesion difficult. If is therefore recommended to apply a proprietary concrete sealer. This should then be painted over with an oil-based paint.

If you are screeding a new concrete floor, it should be wood floated and allowed to dry for at least 28 days before painting. To test if the floor is dry, securely tape a small piece of plastic to the surface. Lift after 24 hours; and if condensation has formed, it is still too damp.

Wood Old floorboards will probably need to be sanded to achieve a good, smooth surface, although a thorough scrubbing is sometimes sufficient. If you are planning to paint the whole surface, you will have to use a primer and universal undercoat in preparation. In addition, exposed nails – which must be hammered flush with the boards – should be coated with a metal primer to avoid rusting.

If the wood has been sealed or varnished, it can be stripped or, once again, sanded. If you are planning to paint the floor surface anyway, sand lightly to provide a key and simply paint with universal undercoat. Your base coat can then be painted on top with minimum fuss. If the floor has been waxed, first clean with sugar soap or a dilute solution of a degreaser.

If there is evidence of wood rot or beetle, treat, or in severe cases replace, the affected wood. Registered pest control companies will advise if necessary.

Vinyl tiles A painted floor is, in many instances, a vast aesthetic improvement on vinyl tiles. But be warned, the glue these tiles leave behind is difficult to remove. Unless you are prepared for a hard task using powerful solvents, it is probably worth getting the floor screed over by a professional.

Cork tiles As long as it is not badly chipped, cork can be successfully painted, providing a particularly successful base for an interesting marbled finish.

CEILINGS

While ceilings in past centuries received great attention, twentieth-century ceilings are frequently neglected. Even the paints we use for ceilings are generally uninspiring to those we use on our walls.

Preparation for a ceiling is largely the same as that for a wall. If it is wooden, follow the preparation required for floorboards. More often than not, special ceiling board (like gypsum plaster board) is used, giving you a good, smooth surface on which to work. However, as ceiling board is often absorbent, a plaster primer is a good idea. Alternatively, apply a 5:1 emulsion/water solution.

WOODWORK

Doors, shutters, window frames, skirting boards, dado and picture rails, as well as other mouldings, are all possible subjects for decorative paint finishes.

If the surface is sound you may be able to overpaint with the minimum of preparation. However, peeling, blistering and uneven paint should always be stripped. Holes and cracks must be repaired with a proprietary wood filler which should be sanded smooth when dry to give a good sound surface.

New wood Even a new surface requires preparation and unless you plan to lime or pickle the wood, it should be painted with a proprietary primer and then universal undercoat. Alternatively, after priming use a one coat paint which does not require undercoats.

Painted wood Having established that your surface is sound, simply clean off all the grime with sugar soap and sand lightly to provide a 'key' for the new paint or decorative treatment.

Varnished wood Provided the surface is in good condition, you can paint with universal undercoat and then apply your required ground or base coat.

FURNITURE

The rules for decorating furniture are, in essence, the same as for any other surface. Dirt must be removed; peeling or flaking paints and varnishes must be scraped or stripped; and any damage must be repaired. As always, proper preparation is essential for a successful finish.

WALLS

Walls provide the largest, most dominant and most obvious surfaces for decorative paint treatments. They are also suitable for just about every technique in this book.

The options for wall treatments are endless. Even once you have furnished and decorated a room, wall colours and effects may be changed to alter atmosphere, mood and style.

Before painting begins, there is some very basic planning which should be done. After all, you need to decide on the effect you want as well as the colour you are going to use. Successful decorating relies as much on your own taste as on understanding the basic practicalities and aesthetics involved.

Planning

Look carefully at the room in question and consider the elements already there. If you have some furniture, soft furnishings, rugs or even a painting you love, you may find these give you the starting point for your basic colour scheme. If not, decide on a plan of action which will result in a harmonious whole.

To a large extent, the style of your furniture and other belongings will dictate which wall treatments will be most appropriate in the room. Natural lighting, basic wall finishes (including the state of the plaster) and existing paint or other wall-coverings will also play an important role.

Light

We know that light affects colour, but we often forget to take this into account when painting a room.

In general, a wall facing a window will show colours in their true brightness, while walls under a window will appear darker. It is sometimes a good idea to paint small test areas both under and opposite windows. If a painted room is light and airy, it will usually be bright too; whereas a poorly lit room appears dark and, if you are not careful, dreary.

Surfaces

The most common internal wall surface is plastered brick.

Dry wall partitions (often constructed from gypsum plasterboard) are found in many timber-frame homes, and they are equally suitable for decorative paint treatments.

There is also no reason why wood panelling should not be dragged with a thin glaze or be painted and then ragged or sponged. Stencilling can also look effective on bare wood.

Paint

If your wall is already painted, it is wise to ascertain what kind of paint was used before you make a final decision regarding a new paint treatment.

Distemper Historically, distemper was a common finish on walls. A mixture of starches, pigments and extenders like whiting, it has a 'chalky' feel. Although you will be unlikely to find distempered walls today, modern distemper is making something of a come back. Although cheap to apply, the most fragile form of distemper – whitewash – has a dusty, chalky surface which creates considerable problems when overcoating with modern paint.

Left: Sponged pillars, stencilling and graceful painted ducks on the wall add charm and colour.
Painted stripes can look like wallpaper (bottom) or may simply add stylish character to a washed wall (below).

To test for existing distemper, run your hand over the surface. Excessive chalkiness is a good indication that it was previously used. A thorough scrub followed by a coat of PVA sealer should enable you to paint over it.

Emulsion Although they are not technically compatible, oil-based glazes can be used over a sound emulsion base, especially if a silk finish has been used previously. If there is any evidence of flaking or peeling, you would be advised to repaint the wall with universal undercoat before going any further.

Eggshell or gloss An oil- or solvent-based paint is more brittle than an emulsion finish and can often be identified by pressing a coin against the surface which should first be dampened. If yours is an eggshell finish, oil-based or scumble glazes may be applied directly on top – providing of course the surface is clean, sound and the original colour is compatible with the glaze. If you have got a gloss surface, you will have to recoat with an eggshell or universal undercoat to get a satisfactory ground.

Note that water-based washes should not be applied over oil-based eggshell or gloss. However, with the increasing availability of water-based eggshell and gloss paints, you should be able to achieve a wider range of finishes. Universal undercoat can also sometimes be used as a satisfactory ground.

Effects

A host of paint techniques are appropriate for walls. They may be used in isolation or in conjunction with one another to create a myriad of magical effects.

Although most of the finishes are dealt with in detail in individual sections, the following breakdown lists the most appropriate finishes for walls and provides an instant guide.

Stippling This age-old technique softens and blends colours and eliminates brush strokes, as well as effectively hiding minor imperfections. It is not a particularly distinguished finish, but is useful when used in conjunction with marbling and other faux finishes. It may also be used to reduce the brushiness or a colourwashed surface. It is commonly used by professionals to prepare surfaces for dragging.

Sponging Often the amateur's first choice, sponging is quick, easy and versatile. Sponging a wall in several shades can help bring a decorating scheme together, although restraint should be used if the colours are bright. This technique is useful for toning down – or enlivening – existing wall colours.

Ragging The current craze for paint techniques seems to have resulted in a rash of ragged rooms, usually in varying shades of peach, pink, apricot and terracotta. This is quite understandable, however, as ragging and rag rolling both produce a good, textured effect which is unobtrusive and elegant. Furthermore, these immensely popular colours are 'warm and human': they help us feel calm, content and secure.

Distressing A lovely effect of wear and tear can be created without the accompanying deterioration of age. This finish looks good with antique and modern furniture alike.

Dragging When it comes to walls, dragging must be well done to create the sophisticated look which flatters the kind of interior John Fowler made famous. The fine stripes of colour it produces look best in a formal setting. It is a good idea to limit dragging to faux panels or smaller areas, for instance, below a dado rail.

Left top: Glazed walls in mottled shades.
Left top centre: Stylishly combed walls.
Left bottom centre: A marbled wall forms the backdrop for naïve trompe l'oeil.
Left: A combination of techniques in several colours over a shocking pink base.

Colourwashing Cheap and easy to do, colourwashing is perfect for country-style homes, both big and small. It looks particularly pretty when combined with the tiny sprig-printed fabrics in the style of Liberty or Laura Ashley.

Rubbing Rubbed walls look best when bold, earthy hues cover a pale pastel base. A rubbed surface has a lovely depth and translucency and is particularly suitable for large rooms.

Spattering Although spattering can be used, quite successfully, in isolation on walls, it is usually more effective when combined with other techniques like rubbing or ragging.

Faux finishes While there is absolutely no reason why walls should not be marbled, tortoiseshelled or treated with any one of the many bravura finishes, it is better to limit the area painted to panels. Alternatively, divide the wall into faux tiles, for a more realistic effect.

Stencilling Any one of the basic paint finishes works well as a base for stencilling although washed, rubbed, subtly sponged or stippled surfaces are particularly suitable.

Above: Rosebud pink was applied to the walls with bunches of ostrich feathers.
Below: Blue sky and clouds in a bathroom create an unworldly ethereal impression.

Murals and trompes l'oeil Walls provide the perfect backdrop for these.

FLOORS

Floors take the greatest hammering of all the surfaces in any home. We walk on them daily and, therefore, they must be practical as well as good-looking.

Most of us have lived with carpets and other conventional floor coverings for so long that the suggestion of a painted floor surface is just a little disconcerting. But it is not as outrageous as it seems. A paint, stain or bleach treatment can be considerably cheaper than a conservative carpet covering. It is also a viable alternative in the event of allergies to house dust, which inevitably gets trapped under carpeting.

At the same time, practicality is not always the deciding factor. Paint will not last as long underfoot as good-quality carpets, tiles or probably even vinyl; but a cheap covering may be visually inferior to an aesthetically well-presented paint finish.

I recently saw a remade art deco house with its concrete stairway covered in white Italian tiles. It looked sterile and new and I could not help wishing that they had been more adventurous and given a fantasy finish such as faux marble a try.

In a house of another style, a painted tread (carpet) or stencilled border, might have been an imaginative alternative.

Above: A beautifully bleached and pickled floor adds to the simple style of a home.
Below: Wonderfully realistic marble effects created on a large floor surface.

Surfaces

Suitable surfaces for painting and staining include wooden floorboards and concrete which has been screeded with cement. Quarry tiles and brick paving could also be painted or stencilled. Wood may be limed or bleached.

Effects

While only a handful of paint techniques are really appropriate for floors, it will largely be the effect you wish to create which will determine your approach.

Marble A myriad of marble effects can be successfully created on floor surfaces. Real marble is usually laid in slabs, so this is the most convincing way to paint it. The technique of floating marble – similar to that used for marbled paper – will create an attractive fossilstone finish. To do this, water, oil colour and turpentine are all splashed over a prepared base. The water disperses the oil and then dries, leaving a lovely mottled effect. Fossilstone marble may also be created by cissing an already blotchy glaze surface.

*Above: This parquetry design was created
by simply staining floorboards.
Right: Stencilling and hand painting.*

Granite Coarse granite is another obvious
finish for floors. Like marbling, it is most
effective in slabs or a chequerboard design.
A credible granite effect can be quickly
created by a combination of sponging and
spattering.

Woodgrain Floors may be combed to simulate wood. Alternatively, this effect may
simply be used to create unusual and interesting patterns. Although specialist combing equipment can entail some cost, combs
cut from thick cardboard, a cork tile or
rubber squeegee make satisfactory substitutes.

Marquetry Wood stains and dyes may be
used to create rich, inlaid effects. Even a
simple chequerboard (parquetry design)
stained in two colours can be most attractive.

Rugs Carpet and trompe l'oeil rugs are the
pièces de résistance for floors. These may
be painted freehand or stencilled. Wooden
floors may be painted a colour, bleached,
pickled or limed; or they may be left with
the gleaming wood as a natural background
to the paint work.

Materials

Paints, stains, dyes and varnishes all have their place in floor decoration.

Gloss and eggshell High-gloss paints may be used for decoration, such as simple, painted rugs. The disadvantage is that this brittle paint does have a tendency to chip. If you want to use an oil-based medium and plan to stencil over it, rather use a solvent-based eggshell or universal undercoat. For stencilling, fast-drying stencil paints are recommended.

Emulsions Although not meant for floor surfaces, emulsion paints can be used, provided you seal the paintwork thoroughly when dry. In fact one of the prettiest stencilled floors I have seen was done in emulsion and sealed with an interior emulsion sealer – and, although it was not in a high-traffic area, it had endured several years of wear without visible deterioration. If you want to use a water-based paint to decorate a floor try using a more robust type, like an exterior paint.

Road paint Although fast drying, road paint is not as hardy a covering as one might think. Its incompatibility with turpentine (it requires special thinners) is also a disadvantage in the domestic situation.

Stains A wide range of wood stains is available from DIY and hardware stores. These are available in natural wood finishes and colours, like green. Also available are the pre-stained varnishes which save you sealing or varnishing the floor once it has been stained.

Dyes Both spirit and water-based dyes are available for a multitude of materials (for example fabric and leather), and most work well on bare wood. Artists' inks are another interesting alternative. It is, however, wise to experiment on an offcut plank before tackling your floor.

Powder pigments An attractive finish can be achieved by colouring your cement screed mix with pigment powders like red iron oxide.

Glazes For marbling and combing, glazes may be used. The surface must, however, be thoroughly sealed once it is dry.

Protection

The key to a successful floor finish is in the final protection it is given. There are numerous varnishes and specialist wood sealers, many of which are suitable.

It is probably best to use a varnish specifically manufactured for floors. These are especially hard-wearing and many are now very quick-drying – some dry in as little as three hours. Yacht varnish may also be used, but it is relatively slow-drying, highly glossy and yellows considerably.

The only products which should not yellow are water-based emulsion- or acrylic-based sealers. The disadvantage of using most water-based products on floor surfaces is that they are not so hard-wearing and you will have to recoat frequently, especially in high-traffic areas.

Below: A simple painted rug painted on natural floorboards.
Bottom: The amazing effect of worn tiles was created by painting over a concrete base.

CEILINGS

There is absolutely no doubt that ceilings are the most neglected surfaces in modern homes. While decorative paint techniques are unlikely to make an instant impact in this area, they can provide renewed inspiration.

Modern neglect of imaginative ceiling finishes is probably due as much to the minimalised proportions of rooms as to a general fear of tackling surfaces in the style of Michelangelo.

Through the ages, ceilings have got lower and lower, and today we are frequently faced with homes only just conforming to building regulations. This means that the average house has a ceiling 2.1 m (8 ft) from floor level.

It is certainly a far cry from the wonderfully large-proportioned rooms commonly found in many British homes which date from the eighteenth and nineteenth centuries.

Historically, one finds beautifully hand-painted and stencilled ceilings as well as gracious steel-pressed ceilings. Old timber-framed buildings frequently boasted generous wooden beams which, left unpainted, needed no further ceiling treatment.

In Europe, we can still see wonderful examples of early ceiling paintings, especially those accomplished by the Renaissance artists. Best known are probably Leonardo da Vinci's enchanting intertwined boughs painted on a vaulted ceiling at Lodovico Sforza's castle in Milan in the fifteenth century and Michelangelo's stunning freehand figures on the ceiling of the Sistine Chapel (1508–1512).

Effects

Accepting the fact that ceilings are usually an area where we take the line of least resistance, there are a few viable alternatives to the modern norm.

Colour Instead of automatically painting every ceiling white, consider a colour. While low-ceilinged rooms definitely do benefit from light ceilings, as long as you keep the shade paler than the walls, you can often safely introduce a touch of colour.

Generally, if a ceiling is very high, it can be visually lowered with a deep warm colour. When it is neither high nor low, pastel tints of warm colours often work well.

Broken colour While colour will remedy many situations, in most cases it will not disguise poor structure or bad finishes. As a result, there are people who employ 'broken colour' instead to act as a camouflage.

A word of caution: while sponging can sometimes do the trick, ragging often draws attention to the problem. At the same time, a ceiling, rag rolled in the same (or fractionally lighter) colour as the walls can give a large room an inviting charm.

Marbling Although physically demanding, domed ceilings benefit from this treatment. Simpler, and yet striking in a formal room, the cornice may also be marbled.

Stencilling Especially effective on beams or as a border.

Mundane white ceilings give way to (below) pretty pastel colours, broken paint treatments like ragging (bottom right); or, if you really want something different, a glamorous starry sky effect (bottom left). All may be achieved with paint.

Hand painting Ceilings in historic homes were painted by professionals. Unless you are a keen artist with aspirations in this area, the hand-painted approach should be avoided by amateurs.

Trompe l'oeil skies If approached in a mood of fun and fantasy, a patchy blue and cloudy-white sky can add charm and even an illusion of space to an informal room. While this idea has classical origins, you do not need to be a great artist to produce convincing results.

Bleaching and liming Wooden ceilings may be given a traditional or fake lime treatment, or they may be 'pickled' with a variety of proprietary bleaches. This gives a soft, mellow look instead of the more usual glowing polyurethane surfaces one sees.

Paint

Ordinary white emulsion paint is probably the most commonly used medium.

Flat oil ceiling paint Cheaper than most other paints, it is underbound to enable one to keep a 'wet edge' while painting. There is no reason why it should not be coloured with a universal tinter.

Gloss paints In addition to flat oil ceiling paint, other oil-based paints like eggshell, can be effective and practical. They are especially useful for steel-pressed ceilings.

Emulsions A matt vinyl emulsion is most frequently used on ceilings. A silk emulsion may also be used, but it will produce a sheen which can tend to highlight imperfections. Also available is an emulsion paint in either matt or silk finishes which fills cracks as you paint.

Glazes For techniques like ragging and marbling, use the same materials recommended for walls. Be prepared for a mess as working upside down with thinned paints is quite a challenge.

Bleaches Oxalic acid, hydrogen peroxide and caustic soda may all be used for bleaching. These are harsh, potentially dangerous agents, and should be handled with the utmost respect. Instead, try proprietary wood bleaches and lighteners.

Right above: This charming and intricate stencilling was used to embellish a ceiling many years ago.
Right: A central ceiling panel painted to look like a blue but cloudy sky.

WOODWORK

Woodwork in many contemporary homes is left in its natural state. In older homes it was usually painted although the modern trend is to strip it to its original form.

If you are lucky enough to have a home with richly toned oak, teak or even oregon pine woodwork, you are unlikely to want to paint it. In fact, if it is painted already, you are more likely to be pulling out paint stripper and heat guns in an endeavour to restore it to its natural state.

You may even feel that it is sacrilege to paint such common wood as pine. If so, now is the time for reassessment.

While some woods should undoubtedly be left unpainted, others have little natural beauty and certainly benefit from paint treatments. However, this does not necessarily mean inferior wood should be automatically coated with layers of gloss paint. Some of the most basic paint techniques provide viable alternatives.

Preparation

The very position of woodwork in the home makes preparation an important factor. Doors and windows, especially, are handled a lot and invariably become scarred with use. Mostly they can be repaired by cleaning and filling, although sometimes you will have to undertake thorough scraping and stripping even if you are going to repaint.

Before new wood can be painted, you will normally have to apply a coat of wood primer and an undercoat. Remember, too, that sealed or varnished wood will have to be sanded to provide a 'key' for the next coat of paint, or overpainted with universal undercoat before painting proper can begin.

Effects

When referring to general woodwork in the home, one looks not only at doors and window frames, but also at skirting boards, dado and picture rails, shutters, wooden architraves and mouldings; as well as bannisters, wooden panels, mantelpiece and fire surrounds.

While the traditional proprietary paints for woodwork are oil-based, gloss and eggshell or satin finishes are now available in water-based alternatives. Decorative paint techniques provide additional interesting and attractive alternatives.

Colour Woodwork provides a perfect framework for a colour-trim within a decorative scheme. This is a good place to introduce contrasts.

Dragging One of the most appropriate decorative paint finishes for woodwork is dragging. Not only is it simple and economical to do, but it is flattering too. Larger areas may be tackled in a combination of techniques: dragging mouldings, rails and stiles, and sponging or stippling the bigger panels.

When dragging woodwork, the rule of thumb is to follow the grain of the wood. Wipe the raised sections of moulding for added effect; or 'antique' by dragging off-white or wiping raw umber over white-painted mouldings.

Left: A pretty peppermint pink kitchen with glazed cupboards which have been dabbed off with paper towel.
Below: A plastic-bagged door.

A colourful coat of paint transforms wooden cupboards in a child's bedroom.

Sponging and ragging Both sponging and ragging are often considered to be good ways of camouflaging unwanted features – which might well extend to some of the woodwork in your home. In a small area, for instance, a common colour which employs just one technique, can add visual harmony to a room.

Both these paint treatments work particularly well on door and cupboard areas; sponging is, however, easier on smaller surfaces like frames and rails. Either may be used in combination with dragging or even solid paint work.

Woodgraining Traditionally, it was quite acceptable – even expected in certain circles – for woodwork to be grained. This was because people wanted expensive-looking woods, but could only afford the cheaper varieties.

Marbling As a fake or fantasy finish, marbling is particularly appropriate on almost all types of woodwork. Wooden fireplace surrounds and mantelpieces also benefit from this technique.

Stencilling On its own, stencilling can enliven the dullest door or cupboard front, irrespective of whether it is applied over paint or bare wood. However, I do like the idea of imitating marquetry and other inlay techniques with wood stains.

Trompe l'oeil Many of us are stricken (usually for economic reasons) with ugly hollow-core doors and very plain cupboards. Instead of sticking on apologetic mouldings deemed to give a panelled look, try your hand at simple trompe l'oeil panels. You will break the flatness of the surface and have an original approach to display.

Above left: Charming hand-painted detail on a front door.
Above right: Fake inlay painted on wooden doors about a century ago.

Paint

We have grown up knowing that gloss paints are meant for woodwork, and with good reason. These paints are generally protective and hard-wearing. Furthermore, this is one place where high-gloss paints can look great.

If your woodwork already has a coat (or more) of gloss paint, provided it is in good condition (clean and sound), you can go ahead and overpaint. If you are faced with new wood and you are lazy – or desperate for immediate results – an exciting modern alternative is the self-undercoating paint which is quick drying.

For decorative paint treatments which require a glaze, you are going to need a low-sheen base: any good-quality undercoat, eggshell or satin wood finish.

FURNITURE

Furniture is a field all of its own. Even the cheapest, most ordinary pieces can benefit from a wide range of treatments ranging from simple sponging to marbling, intricate hand painting and gilding.

I doubt if there is any paint technique which has not been used for furniture. Even colourwashing (which I would put at the top of the list of inappropriate treatments) has been used quite effectively to decorate big items like free-standing wardrobes and expansive table tops.

Painted furniture is found everywhere: in mansions, cottages and even museums throughout the world. Traditional American folk furniture, Scandinavian country furniture, painted Victorian furniture especially from the Arts and Crafts period, as well as the exuberantly decorated pieces painted by Bloomsbury figures, all give inspiration. Not to forget furniture painted in ancient Egypt and China thousands of years ago.

While professional antiquing and glorious gilding may be beyond your scope, there are some superb and simple treatments which not only add colour, interest and texture, but also protect surfaces and disguise inferior wood and workmanship. Furthermore, a popular paint treatment used on a collection of ill-assorted pieces can be an incredibly simple means of unifying a room. Just remember to co-ordinate the colours you choose.

What to paint
Most furniture can be painted, although good wood should respectfully be left. If a piece was previously painted with high-gloss paint, you will either have to rub it down to form a 'key' for new paint, or you will have to overpaint.

Furniture which has been oiled and waxed will have to be stripped. Although varnished pieces can be overpainted with universal undercoat, it is preferable to strip these too. Melamine and other laminates can be painted, but again, they must be rubbed with coarse sandpaper to provide a 'key' for the new treatment. New wood should be primed.

Finishes
Faced with old, battered or even an uninspiring new piece of furniture, it is quite likely that a good, solid coat of gloss paint may seem like the easiest solution. While it will give some cheap pieces an instant facelift, colourful high-gloss paint is not the best solution as there are so many more sophisticated and elegant alternatives.

Antique finishes Antiqued furniture may be lumped together in a rather nebulous category ranging from pieces made to look dull and worn with age to highly polished, lacquered or gilded items modelled in the old tradition. Old furniture may be restored and given one of many antique finishes to add authenticity, while new furniture may be treated to instantly age it.

Fake fantasy finishes A range of marbled, fossiled, malachite, lapis lazuli and tortoiseshell finishes are appropriate and fun for furniture. Bambooing, so fashionable in early nineteenth-century England, is another alternative. These finishes may be totally imitative or purely decorative.

Painted decoration Hand painting and stencilling may be used to decorate any number of pieces. Chair backs, table tops, chests and cupboards all present perfect surfaces.

Marbling enhances an art deco-style screen and complementary lampstand.

Effects

Like all other surfaces, the effect you want to achieve will determine the techniques you opt to use.

Stippling A gently stippled ground provides a particularly pretty surface for hand-painted or stencilled decoration.

Sponging A useful trick to help bring a décor scheme together is to sponge the colours found in the curtains and upholstery onto the furniture in the room. Simple sponging may even be used as part of a process to antique pieces, provided soft, classical colours are used. Soft sponging in pastel shades looks good as a background for stencils.

Colourwashing Simple pine furniture can benefit from this technique, although to be effective it should be confined to larger surfaces. It is most appealing when several layers are washed over one another.

Rubbing Colour rubbing is particularly useful when antiquing a piece of furniture.

Dragging Although a fairly formal finish, dragging suits the simple lines of many modern pieces. It can be used in combination with other techniques.

Furniture is a perfect foil for the more popular and dramatic paint effects, especially hand painting (above), marbling and dragging. I have found that white marble (below) is especially simple.

Stencilling The beauty of stencils are that they can be used on painted surfaces or on wood. For instance, a rich-toned country cupboard could be decorated without losing the charm and lustre of the natural wood finish.

Spattering The speckled spots spattering achieves can add life and interest to chipboard tables and other plain pieces. It is particularly effective when a porphyry finish is required; while some professionals use the technique with a range of others to achieve a beautifully original and stylish look. The addition of gold or silver veining creates a wonderfully exotic faux marble.

Marbling Built-in cupboards, table tops and panels given a faux marble treatment will immediately inject new life and elegance to a room.

Vinegar graining A light-hearted finish, vinegar graining is great for cheap pine pieces. It is quick and easy and although traditionally done in earthy colours, can be translated into any colour of the rainbow. Just remember to varnish well for protection.

Woodgraining Soft woods were traditionally grained to imitate the hard, expensive woods like mahogany and walnut. This is not a particularly fashionable technique nowadays, but it does have its place on cheap, uninspiring pieces.

Right: A lick of mid-blue satinwood paint gives plain pine furniture a brand new look. Placed on the cleverly painted 'rug', it becomes a dining area with a well-defined space.

Below: A bedside table takes on its own look of modern impressionistic marbling. First, two colours were applied and smudged into each other: then the surface was spattered with two more colours. Finally, silver veins and spatters were added.

Bambooing Chairs and tables with turned legs can benefit from a faux bamboo treatment, although I prefer to restrict this technique to picture frames. An interesting variation I saw recently was an insipid bamboo chair painted and them 'bambooed' in fantasy colours to give it new life.

Liming Fake liming, relief rubbing and grain rubbing may all be used for furniture. This family of techniques is particularly useful for antiquing carved furniture.

Lining Both fine and edge lining are employed to define the edges of furniture and basically finish them off. It is particularly helpful when a piece has been dragged, ragged, stippled or sponged. As their names imply, fine lining is the addition of thin lines to highlight features, while edge lining uses broader lines painted around the edges. Swordliners, available from specialist art shops, are particularly useful for lining. You can cheat by using a felt-tipped pen.

Objects

A host of small items, like boxes, trays, lamp stands and picture frames can all benefit from decorative paint treatments. This is where you can really go to town with techniques like malachiting, tortoiseshelling and lapis lazuli.

In fact, it is often a good idea to practise on smaller items before tackling larger pieces of furniture.

MATERIALS, TOOLS AND EQUIPMENT

Much of the equipment required for decorative paint techniques will be found in the basic tool kit most householders already have. In addition, certain specialist tools and brushes will assist in the creation of these effects.

Paints, too, will often be located on familiar DIY or hardware store shelves, and glazes may be mixed using common domestic ingredients. Ultimately, however, the materials, tools and equipment you need will depend on the techniques you plan to tackle.

TECHNIQUE TOOL BOX

Stationery and hardware shops have always fascinated me. I am neither an artist nor a handyman, yet I will spend hours exploring the shelves in search of inspiration.

Specialist art shops are a new discovery to me and fast becoming a new obsession. Consequently, gathering the essential tools for an amateur decorative painter has been an absolute pleasure.

You will not need everything featured on these pages, unless you are planning to try every technique. So look again at the information given in the relevant sections before you go shopping.

Brushes
A selection of ordinary domestic paintbrushes is essential for applying undercoats and base coats (your ground). A small brush (25 mm/1 in) is useful for smaller areas while a good, wide (at least 100 mm/4 in) brush is suitable for colourwashing. A good-quality block brush may be used for dragging. Alternatively, cut bristles from a ragged old brush to imitate the real thing. Buy the best you can afford as bristles do tend to shed from cheaper varieties.

Artists' brushes should include a hake brush, manufactured for watercolour painting and sometimes used by potters for applying glazes; and a selection of ordinary soft-haired brushes useful for painting detail like marble veins and bamboo features. A swordliner is a good idea if you plan to line furniture.

A good selection of specialist brushes are available from DIY or hardware stores, including stencil, stippling and badger brushes. An old toothbrush may be used for spattering.

Soft tools
Marine sponges are an invaluable aid and rags a necessity, regardless of the technique you are tackling. Mutton cloth, or stockinette, sometimes used for ragging, is a must for cleaning-up operations. You should also have a selection of other rags, including old sheeting, as well as a good supply of plastic shopping bags. Goose feathers are useful for veining in marbling.

Hard tools
While specialist tools like steel and rubber combs, as well as overgrainers are available from specialist decorating shops, amateurs can make do with handy alternatives like plastic Afro combs, home-made rubber squeegees or cardboard combs.

Household scourers, wire wool and, of course ordinary wire brushes may be used for distressing.

Other equipment
A craft, hobby or utility trimming knife may be used to cut stencil sheeting.

Useful aids for preparation include masking tape, a plumb line, buckets, bowls and saucers, wide-necked bottles, old plastic measuring spoons, as well as newspaper, sandpaper, pencils and felt-tip pens.

Paint
Standard paints play a large role in decorative painting, as essential ingredients in glazes and washes and, more especially, when it comes to preparing the surface. Your base coat (or ground) must be clean and sound and it should be compatible with the medium to be used over it. So if you are planning to use an oil-based or scumble glaze, the surface should first be painted with an oil-based paint.

Oil-based or gloss paints Avoid paints with a high-gloss finish, and use an eggshell or satinwood finish for your ground. A good-quality undercoat has a nice matt finish and it may be overpainted or used as a ground. Most gloss paints are alkyd based although some have a modified alkyd base. An advantage of non-drip paints, which are thixotropic, is that they even themselves out on the surface giving a smooth surface free of brush strokes.

1. A selection of domestic paint brushes and a mohair roller for preparation and colourwashing.
2. Tools for woodgraining and combing. From top left, clockwise: triangular comb, heart-grainer, steel comb, graduated rubber comb, Afro comb.
3. Miscellaneous tools for ragging, sponging, stippling and vinegar painting. From top left, clockwise: old cotton sheeting, marine sponge, plastic shopping bag, a cork, plasticine, stippling brush, stockinette.
4. Stencilling equipment includes brushes, foam applicator, knives, various types of stencil sheeting and masking tape.
5. A goose feather and several artists' brushes including a liner and swordliner (right).
6. Hake brushes (right) and badger softening brushes.
7. Brushes for dragging include an old brush with bristles cut out (top), a flogger (right) and a block brush (bottom).
8. Wire scourer and sandpaper, useful for distressing.

Read the manufacturer's instructions on the tin prior to application as special factors might apply: for instance check for drying times and remember that if you mix the paint these could well be affected. Non-drip paints will temporarily lose their gel consistency when diluted with turpentine or even with tinters. If allowed to stand for eight hours or more, they should regain their original consistency.

Emulsions Water-based emulsion paints may be used for several techniques including colourwashing and sponging. Matt, satin and silk finishes are suitable. Pure acrylic paint, sold to artists for priming canvas, is useful for small surfaces.

(Both eggshell and gloss finishes are now available in water-based suspensions).

Base paints The transparent and translucent bases (for emulsions and gloss paints) used for custom mixing paint are particularly useful for decorative paint techniques as they allow colour to show through a delicate film. The results are quite sheer and radiant, and you can effectively build up colour as you would with a wash. Note that these paints are not on the shelves but may be found at paint mixing centres within DIY and décor stores.

Colour

Paints are available in a substantial range of colours, either ready-mixed or custom-mixed to your choice. However, you can often achieve wonderful results by mixing your own colours into paints, washes and glazes.

Artists' oils Available from specialist art shops and some hardware stores, artists' oils enable you to achieve a huge colour range. They may only be used to colour oil-based paints and glazes; and they also take a long time to dry. Note that oils made with natural dyes are considerably more expensive than those made with synthetic colour.

Universal tinters Stains known as universal tinters are particularly useful for colouring paints and glazes as they are

---

PREPARING YOUR SURFACE

Before you tackle any paint finish, you must ensure your surface is properly prepared, otherwise anything you put on top could simply be wasted. This guide will help you when faced with a bare surface to decorate.

WALLS AND CEILINGS	PRIMER	UNDERCOAT
New plaster or plasterboard	one coat of thinned emulsion OR alkali-resisting primer	not needed only under some gloss paints
Good, sound painted plaster	one coat of thinned emulsion on any bare areas	not needed
Lining paper/ anaglypta	one coat of thinned emulsion if using oil-based top coats	only under some gloss paints
WOOD		
Bare soft wood or building boards	wood primer (apply knotting first over resinous areas or knots)	only under some gloss paints
Bare hardwood	universal primer or aluminium primer	only under some gloss paints
Good, sound, previously painted wood	not needed	not needed except under some gloss finishes
METAL		
Radiators	metal primer (if bare metal)	not needed
Metal window frames	metal primer on any bare areas	universal undercoat

---

compatible with gloss paints and emulsions. You can buy them in tubes from specialist decorating stores.

To tint custom-coloured paints (like the instore mixing machine ranges) manufacturers have a wider choice of stains. Some paint stores will sell small quantities to customers, but because they are decanted from a supplier's machine (rather than pre-packed for resale) you may have to supply your own container. Remember that these tints are relatively expensive but that only small quantities are required.

Pigment powders Pigments available in powder form are particularly useful for colouring washes and essential for vinegar graining. Red iron oxide, green oxide, black oxide and yellow ochre are only available through specialist suppliers, while a larger range of pigments, stains and oxides (like blue cobalt oxide and green chromium oxide) are available from potters' suppliers.

Before you colour paint, test the materials for compatibility as many of the avail-

able powders are water soluble.

Artists' acrylics Quick-drying acrylic paint is useful for tinting emulsion paints.

Solvents

The most common solvents are water (used in conjunction with emulsion paints and universal stainers) and turpentine. For cleaning brushes and other tools used for oil-based paints, white spirit is an accepted solution. However, even more effective are degreasers (like Polyclens), potent solvents which allow all residue to be rinsed off with water after cleaning.

A thinner is another solvent – compatible, for instance with lacquer. It is also useful as a first-aid solution for brushes which have not been properly cleaned.

For diluting paint and mixing home-made glazes, turpentine oil (sometimes sold for medicinal use), is a successful option. Although it is considerably more expensive than white spirit, it smells better and is less harsh on the hands.

Oils

Linseed oil is a usual ingredient in home-made glazes. Most commonly used is boiled linseed, although purified linseed oil and other artists' mediums are sometimes preferred. Raw linseed oil is also available but this should never be boiled at home.

Note that boiled linseed oil does tend to yellow on oxidation and it retards drying.

Driers

The use of linseed oil and pure artists' oil colours (both of which slow down drying times) seems to be the most common reason for using a fast-drying medium with decorative paint techniques. If you do wish to add a quick drying medium to your preparation, it is worth checking in art shops for a proprietary substance. Winsor and Newton manufacture a liquid alkyd resin with the brand name Liquin, a product which is available in many countries. Not only does this help speed up the drying time, it also improves the brushstrokes and increases transparency. It is especially good for glazing.

Sealers

Varnish The most commonly used sealer is polyurethane. A clear varnish is useful, and, by tinting, it can be given added depth like lacquer. However, polyurethane does yellow, which sometimes causes major problems. If you are working with 'dirty' colours, this does not matter; but if you are closely colour co-ordinating a surface finish, it does. Take special care if you are sealing greys or shades of blue as they will tend to turn green.

Yacht varnish High-gloss yacht varnish is tough and hard-wearing, but it yellows excessively and so should generally be avoided.

PVA sealer PVA sealer, such as Unibond, is useful because it does not yellow and, although water-based, may be used to seal oil-based glazes. However, it is meant as an undercoat board sealer and is not the perfect solution.

Acrylic varnish A water-based acrylic varnish may be used successfully over emulsions, gloss paints or glazes. It does not yellow and provides a hard-wearing clear gloss, satin or matt finish.

Note that acrylic varnish should not really be diluted as it will tend to lose its film, however you can risk a maximum dilution of 25 per cent water if absolutely necessary.

Solvent-based glazecoat A decorators' glazecoat, manufactured for sealing textured surfaces and hot, steamy rooms like kitchens and bathrooms, is also available. White spirit should be used to dilute and to clean brushes.

Lacquer Although lacquer is quick-drying and does not yellow, it contains strong (thinner-based) solvents and is not compatible with all painted surfaces. It is also highly inflammable.

Materials for cleaning

Brushes used for water-based paints and acrylics should be washed immediately in hot, soapy water; while those used for oil paints must be cleaned in white spirit or a more potent degreaser like Polyclens. If using turpentine, wipe the brushes dry after soaking and then wash in hot soapy water. If using a degreaser, the paint residue will come away under running water.

If you forget to clean a brush and it gets clogged with thick, sticky paint, soak it in a proprietary brush restorer then clean in the usual way.

Glazes

Many decorative paint techniques rely on glazes for their success. Most frequently used are oil-based or scumble glazes, although emulsion glazes are occasionally a viable alternative.

There are numerous recipes for glazes, and, rather like cooking, practise makes perfect. I have watched various professionals mix their glazes dozens of times, always adding a bit of this and a bit of that, altering their basic ingredients to suit the job. The message here is that you should not be afraid to experiment.

Artists have used glazes since time immemorial: usually consisting of a mixture of oil colour, linseed oil and solvent to thin the mixture and speed drying time. Decorative painters use similar glazes adding eggshell or matt varnish as well.

Several companies manufacture a basic glaze preparation to which you add colour and solvent (turpentine or white spirit).

Note that the furniture scumble sold for finishing off raw wood and chipboard edges has nothing in common with scumble glaze. The common terminology can be a problem and I have met several people who have been sold furniture scumble in error.

Making glazes

To make a good standard glaze you will need a collection of bowls and saucers; a couple of stubby paintbrushes for stirring; and your paint and other ingredients.

To mix, empty a small amount of paint into a small bowl; combine thoroughly with your chosen colourant. In an open-necked bottle or larger bowl, mix this coloured paint with the rest of the eggshell; then add linseed oil, and gradually the turpentine. If you need more colour, mix with untainted paint in your original small bowl and then add to the mixture. If you throw it straight into the half-mixed glaze, you may find it does not combine as readily.

Remember to make a note of quantities and colours added so you can mix more glaze if necessary. It is preferable to have a little too much as most mixtures can be kept for a limited period of time. To use a commercial scumble glaze it is usual to add equal quantities of paint and white spirit.

Technical Terms

For the average home decorator, the paint market has exploded over the last 20 years, with a bewildering array of products on the shelves. Nonetheless, paints still fall basically into two groups: emulsion paints – which are basically water solvent, and oil- or solvent-based paints, which need to be thinned or cleaned with a solvent such as turpentine or white spirit.

Both types contain pigments, usually white (which used to be lead based) and other colours. The pigments are bonded together and to the surface being painted by various resins, usually synthetic ones. In solvent-based paints, the resin binder is dissolved in solvent which enables you to brush on a very smooth coat. As the solvent evaporates, the paint hardens by oxidation. Emulsions work on the same principle, except the paint droplets are dispersed in water. As the water dries, the paint hardens.

HINTS

● Glazes containing varnish tend to form a thick skin after several weeks.

● Linseed oil retards drying and may yellow over time.

● If glaze is applied too thickly, it can form a surface skin which prevents it drying out thoroughly and leaves it tacky.

● When applying acrylic varnish, brush it out well as careless dribbles can cause discoloration.

Most of the technical terms in paint manufacture refer to the resinous binders. In oil paints they are alkyds, in emulsions they are based on vinyl or acrylic which are combined with other chemicals. Once these materials – known as monomers – are mixed together, they become polymers, a word which describes most plastics – and these polymers are also excellent paint binders.

Apart from pigments and binders, paints also contain additives or extenders to add other qualities such as ensuring the paint stores well or that the ingredients don't separate in the tin. Non-drip paints have additives which make the paint thixotropic, or gel-like.

In recent years, most oil-based paints with their glossy, eggshell or satin finishes, are now produced in water-based versions. This makes them odour-free and easier to apply. It also makes brush cleaning simpler. However, oil-based or solvent-based paints are still regarded as longer-lasting, tougher and more resilient than their water-based counterparts.

Whatever the constituents of a paint, the surface can be varied by altering the proportion of pigment to resin. More pigment and less resin and you have a matt surface; roughly equal parts and the surface will tend to be glossy. High pigment content means good coverage, whereas high resin content gives a stronger and easier to clean finish.

Recipes for home-made glazes

Standard scumble glaze
2 parts oil-based eggshell paint
2 parts boiled linseed oil
1 part white spirit
Tinters or artists' oils

Especially good for ragging, dragging and marbling.

Author's transparent glaze
2 parts transparent paint base (from in-store mixing machine)
1–2 parts purified linseed oil
1 part turpentine oil
Artists' oils for colour

Start with one part linseed oil and gradually add more if desired.

Ragging glaze
10 parts eggshell or satin finish (2.5 litres)
10 parts turpentine (2.5 litres)
1 part boiled linseed oil (250 ml/1 cup)
Tinters

Oil-based alternative glaze
4 parts eggshell (a colour or tinted)
4 parts clear matt varnish
4 parts white spirit
1 part boiled linseed oil

Sponge glaze
4 parts eggshell
2 parts turpentine
1 part boiled linseed oil

Useful for sponging off.

Glaze rub
3 parts white spirit
2 parts eggshell (a colour or tinted)
2 parts boiled linseed oil

Good for rubbing on walls.

Oil-free gloss glaze
2 parts eggshell (a colour or tinted)
1 part turpentine oil or white spirit

Good for sponging on.

Tortoiseshell gilp
4 parts clear matt varnish
2 parts white spirit
1 part boiled linseed oil
Raw sienna artists' oil colour
Drier (optional)

Liming gilp
500 ml polyurethane matt varnish
250 ml white eggshell
1 tbsp boiled linseed oil

Paint on and then gently rub off before completely dry.

Water-based glaze
2 parts emulsion
2 parts water
1 part acrylic varnish

Milk varnish
1 part matt varnish
1 part white spirit
White eggshell (a touch)

Tinted varnish
1 part matt varnish
1 part white spirit
Tinters or artists' oils

Vinegar paint
125 ml (4 fl oz) malt vinegar
1 tbsp powder pigment
1 tsp brown sugar
Squeeze dishwashing liquid

COMMON PAINTING PROBLEMS

Providing you follow the instructions in this book carefully, and prepare your surface well first, you should avoid any of the following problems. However, here are the most common ones, the reasons they occur and the remedy.

Drips, runs and sags
These are caused by an uneven application of paint and often occur with oil-based paints which have not been brushed out thoroughly. Drips are also common when applying paint to mouldings or uneven surfaces where paint accumulates. Check paint as you go and brush out any drips at this stage. If the surface has already dried with any drips, you will need to sand it down and repaint.

Flaking or Peeling
This happens when paint loses adhesion with its base. It can also occur when there is surface expansion or contraction. Peeling often starts at a joint or split in the paint. To correct, strip the paint, ensure the surface is dry and thoroughly rub down before repainting.

Blistering
This usually occurs when the top coat does not adhere to a base coat. Sometimes it is because of trapped damp. If the blisters are occasional, remove them, rub down the edges. More serious blistering will need stripping right back. Check that there is no major damp problem before continuing.

Crazing
This can also happen when the under and top coats do not adhere well. May need stripping right back if the problem is severe. If not, gently rub down the top coat.

USEFUL ADDRESSES

All of the following DIY stores stock a wide range of paints and associated products. Most will be able to supply other items such as pre-cut stencil kits. All have outlets across the country. The head offices, below, will be able to advise you of a branch in your locality.

Do-It-All Ltd
Falcon House
The Minories
Dudley
West Midlands
DY2 8PG
0384 456456

Homebase Ltd
Beddington House
Wallington
Surrey
081–784 7200

Texas Homecare Ltd
Homecharm House
Park Farm
Wellingborough
Northants
NN8 6XA
0933 679679

Wickes
120–138 Station Road
Harrow
Middlesex
HA1 2QB
081–863 5696

Specialist decorating suppliers include:

J. W. Bollom
13 Theobalds Road
London
WC1X 8FN
071–242 0313

and

314–316 Old Brompton Road
London
SW5 9JH
071–370 3252

Foxell and James Ltd
57 Farringdon Road
London
EC1M 3JB
071–405 0152

E. Milner Oxford Ltd
Glanville Road
Cowley
Oxford
OX4 2DB
0865 718171

Paint Service Co Ltd
19 Eccleston Street
London
SW1 9WX
071–730 6408

There are also various advisory centres set up by the major manufacturers:

Dulux Paints
ICI Paints Division
Wexham Road
Slough
Berks

The Dulux Colour Centre Studio
PO Box 2581
London
N11 3HR
or telephone the Dulux Advice Centre
0753 550555

Eurostudio (for stencils)
Unit 4 Southdown Ind Estate
Southdown Road
Harpenden
Herts

MANUFACTURERS

Brodie & Middleton Ltd
68 Drury Lane
London
WC2B 5SP
071–836 3289

Craig & Rose plc
172 Leith Walk
Edinburgh
EH6 5EB
031–554 1131

Daler-Rowney Ltd
12 Percy Street
London
W1A 2BP
071–636 8241

Potmolen Paint
27 Woodcock Ind Estate
Warminster
Wiltshire
BA12 9DX
0985 213960

J. H. Ratcliffe and Co
135a Linaker Street
Southport
PR8 5DF
0704 537999

Winsor & Newton
51 Rathbone Place
London
W1P 1AB
071–636 4231

AUSTRALIA
Bristol Decorator Centres
456 Enoggera Road
Alderley 4051
Brisbane QLD
07–536 1044

Bristol Decorator Centres
4/552 Church Street
Parramatta 2150
Sydney NSW
02–630 2851

Leo's Decorators (VIC) Pty Ltd
119 McKinnon Road
McKinnon 3204
McKinnon VIC
03–578 4465

The Paint Pot Decorating Centres Pty Ltd
636 Goodwood Road
Daw Park 5041
Adelaide SA
08–276 9828

Paul's Paint & Decor Centre
57 Dixon Road
Rockingham 6168
Perth WA
09–592 3440

NEW ZEALAND
Levene & Company
Branches Auckland wide

Major Decorating
Branches New Zealand wide

PWF Decor Centre
Branches New Zealand wide

Resene Color Shops
45 shops, Whangerai–Invercargill

GLOSSARY

Acetate Transparent film used for making stencils.

Acrylic Versatile water-based paint which is waterproof when dry.

Acrylic varnish Transparent sealer which will not yellow.

Antiquing Process used to simulate wear and tear on surfaces.

Badger brush Soft-haired brush made from badger hair used for blending and softening. Especially useful for marbling and other bravura techniques.

Bravura technique/effect Ambitious (sometimes brilliant) paint effect.

Bridge Thin piece left once stencil has been cut out.

Cissing Effect created when solvent is spattered onto a wet painted surface.

Combing Technique originally developed for woodgraining where combs are 'dragged' through glaze for effect.

Cornice Moulding between ceiling and wall.

Dado Area of wall below a moulded or painted dado rail. Also called the dadofield. Often broken into panels.

Dado rail Rail originating in the eighteenth century as a chair rail which prevented damage to walls.

Distemper Mixture of whiting and starch traditionally used to wash interior walls.

Distressing Simulation of wear and tear on any surface. Also the technique of breaking up the ground for marbling.

Eggshell Oil or water based paint with a low-sheen finish. Paints described as satinwood are similar.

Emulsion Water-based paint with a matt to high sheen finish. Also available in a solid form for ceilings and walls.

Faux finish Fake finish achieved with decorative paint techniques, including marbling, tortoiseshelling and malachiting.

Fossilstone Stone effect created by cissing or floating marble. Also called fossilstone marbling.

Fresco A traditional and highly specialised method of painting where watercolours are laid on the surface before the plaster is dry.

Frieze Decorative border above the cornice or close to the ceiling. Also found around door and window openings.

Gilp Mixture of linseed oil and varnish used for techniques including tortoiseshelling. An old name for glaze was 'megilp'.

Glaze Transparent or semi-transparent medium which may be emulsion or oil-based.

Gloss A shiny finish obtained most usually from a gloss paint whether oil- or water-based. Also applicable to varnish.

Gouache Opaque watercolour commonly used in commercial and graphic design.

Granite Speckled granular crystalline rock.

Ground Base coat for most decorative paint techniques.

Hake brush Soft watercolour paintbrush, with hake (fish)-shaped hair. May be used as a softener. Sometimes made from wolf hair.

Liming Traditional technique employed to lighten the grain of wood.

Lining Technique used to finish furniture with thin lines.

Mylar Transparent film used for stencilling.

Palette Board used for mixing paints.

Pickling Technique used to bleach wood.

Pigment Colouring matter used as paint or dye.

Polyurethane Synthetic resin used in some paints and varnish.

Porphyry Hard rock composed of red and white crystals. Quarried in Egypt in ancient times.

Satinwood A commercial name for an eggshell type finish. Available in an oil-based and water-based type.

Screed Cement finish laid over concrete floors.

Scumble glaze Transparent oil glaze.

Skirting Trim, usually made of wood, between wall and floor.

Stile The vertical part of a piece framing a panel.

Stippling Technique used to soften and blend colour, eliminating brush strokes.

Stockinette, or mutton cloth. Coarse cloth used for cleaning up and ragging techniques.

Swordliner Paintbrush used for lining furniture.

Thixotropic Term used for paint which returns to gel state after mixing. For example, non-drip gloss.

Trompe l'oeil Painting which deceives the eye.

Vinegar graining Another term for vinegar painting, a cheap and simplified version of woodgraining.

White spirit A cheap (and inferior) turpentine substitute, used for thinning and brush cleaning.

Whitewash A distemper paint made from whiting (usually chalk), size and water.

Whiting A chalky product used with starch to make distemper.

FURTHER READING

Barnett, Helen and Smith, Susy, *Stencilling*, Ward Lock Limited, London, 1987.

Bawden, Juliet, *The Creative Book of Decorative Painting*, Salamander Books, London, 1988.

Better Homes and Gardens (Editorial Staff), *New Decorating Book*, Meredith Corporation, Des Moines, Iowa, 1981.

Bishop, Adele and Lord, Cile, *The Art of Decorative Stencilling*, Viking Press, New York, 1976.

Blake, Jill, *How to Solve Your Interior Design Problems*, Hamlyn, London, 1986. (Revised edition, Penguin, 1985.)

Blake, Wendon, *The Colour Book*, Watson-Guptill, New York, 1981.

Brown, Erica, *Interior Views: Design at its Best*, Thames and Hudson, London, 1980.

Conran, Terence, *New House Book*, Conran Octopus, London, 1985.

Creative Home Decorating, Ward Lock Ltd, London, 1988.

Davies, Keeling, Trowbridge, *Fantasy Finishes*, Macdonald Orbis, London, 1989.

Fisher, Rosie, *Painting Furniture*, Macdonald Orbis, London, 1988.

Fraser, Bridget (Editor), *Stencilling: A Design and Source Book*, The Miller Press, London, 1987.

Gilliat, Mary, *The Decorating Book*, Michael Joseph, London, 1981.

Gilliat, Mary, *Colour Your Home*, Octopus, London, 1985.

Gray, Linda, *Room for Change*, Thames Macdonald, London, 1988.

Green, Caroline, *The Creative Book of Stencilling Designs*, Salamander Books, London, 1990.

Halse, A. O., *The Use of Colour in Interiors*, McGraw Hill, London, 1978.

Hunt, Belinda, *Decorative Paint Finishes*, Ebury Press, London, 1987.

Innes, Jocasta, *Living in Style*, Ebury Press, London, 1984.

Innes, Jocasta, *Paintability*, Weidenfeld and Nicolson, London, 1986.

Innes, Jocasta and Blake, Jill, *The Conran Beginner's Guide to Decorating*, Conran Octopus, London, 1987.

Innes, Jocasta and Gray, Linda, *The Complete Book of Decorating Techniques*, Macdonald Orbis, London, 1987.

Innes, Jocasta, *The New Paint Magic*, Frances Lincoln Ltd, London, 1992.

Jenkins, Jo-An, *Decorating Furniture*, Pelham Books, London, 1984.

Leicht, Hermann, *History of the World's Art*, Spring Books, London, 1983.

Le Grice, Lyn, *The Art of Stencilling*, Crown Publishers, London, 1987.

McCloud, Kevin, *Kevin McCloud's Decorating Book*, Dorling Kindersley, London, 1990.

McGowan, Johan and DuBern, Roger (Editors), *The Book of Home Restoration*, Ebury Press, London, 1985.

Niesewand, Nonie, *The Complete Interior Designer*, Macdonald & Co., London, 1984.

Osborne, Harold (Editor), *The Oxford Companion to the Decorative Arts*, Oxford University Press, Oxford, 1985.

Painting in Oils, Mitchell Beazley, London, 1983.

Peverill, Sue, *The Fabric Decorator*, Macdonald, London, 1988.

Radford, Penny, *Surfaces and Finishes*, Macmillan, London, 1984.

Saint George, Amelia, *The Stencil Book*, Conran Octopus, London, 1988.

Sargent, W., *The Enjoyment and Use of Colour*, Dover Publications, New York, 1964.

Seligman, Patricia, *Painting Murals*, Macdonald Orbis, London, 1987.

Sloan, Annie and Gwynn, Kate, *The Complete Book of Decorative Paint Techniques*, Ebury Press, London, 1992.

Spencer, Andrea, *Paint Techniques*, Conran Octopus, London, 1986.

Spencer, Stuart, *Marbling*, Ward Lock Limited, London, 1987.

Sutcliffe, John, *Decorating Magic*, Frances Lincoln Ltd, London, 1992.

Taylor, A., *Making the Most of Colour in the Home*, Avco Publishers, London, 1968.

The Dictionary of Colours for Interior Decoration, British Colour Council, London, 1949.

Verity, E., *Colour*, Lesley Frewin, London, 1967.

Visser, Jill and Flinn, Michael, *Stencilling Techniques for Interiors, Furniture and Objects*, Macdonald Orbis, London, 1988.

Walker, Aidan, *Wood Polishing and Finishing Techniques*, Ebury Press, London, 1985.

Warrender, Carolyn and Strickland, Tessa, *Carolyn Warrender's Book of Stencilling*, Andre Deutsch, London, 1988.

Wilson, Althea, *Paint Works*, Century Hutchinson, London, 1988.

INDEX